MW01229167

EVOLVING

My Transformation from Brokenness to Abundance

T. RENEÉ SMITH

T. Reneé Smith
c/o iSuccess Consulting, Inc.
3645 Marketplace Blvd., Suite 130-51
Atlanta, Georgia 30344

www.treneesmith.com / www.theceo.life / www.isuccessconsulting.com

Dedication

I dedicate this book, first and foremost, to the most wonderful husband in the world. It amazes me how your love is pure and long-lasting. You have no idea how your stability and consistency have given me the freedom to pursue my passions and purpose. Your integrity encourages me to continuously evolve into the woman, wife, mother, and CEO I was meant to be.

Thank you for loving me during the difficult times and always giving of yourself, sacrificially.

To every woman out there who has doubted yourself, sabotaged your life or relationships without knowing it, held yourself hostage to your past and mistakes, I dedicate this book to you. Today, your process of evolving begins.

Acknowledgments

A great big heartfelt thank you to my children. You are constantly teaching me patience, unconditional love, compassion, and empathy. You remind me to always dream big and stay true to myself. To my parents and brother, thank you for always being there to love and support me. I am who I am because of the sacrifices you made for me.

To my team, you make everything I do possible. Thank you for seeing my vision, believing in me, and having the courage to step out in faith. To all of those who have helped me on this journey, including clients, coaches, teachers, trainers, mentors, friends and family, I honor and appreciate you, and I will forever be grateful.

To my editor, Candice L. Davis, words alone can't express my gratitude to you for encouraging me to tell my story and step into my purpose. Thank you.

Finally, but definitely not least, I give this book back to God, as He has given it to me to share with you.

Contents

Breaking free from your past and going through the process of evolving to fully embrace your authentic self is the greatest gift you can give yourself.

T. RENEÉ SMITH

The Beginning of My Evolution

One New Year's Eve, I sat and reflected on what happened in the last twelve months. Another year had gone by, and I was feeling stuck and alone. As I journaled, I realized I wasn't happy, and worse, I was writing the same thing I had written at the beginning of the last two years.

I felt like I was trapped on a never-ending treadmill. My husband and I still had the same arguments. My business still ran from feast to famine and back again. I was trying to understand my kids and their raging hormones as they went through puberty. And for reasons I couldn't understand, the fat on my belly wasn't just magically disappearing and my home didn't look like the interior design pictures I had saved in Pinterest. What was happening to my life?

I was sick and tired of being sick and tired. In that moment, I decided that twelve months later my life would look totally different. I decided to design the life I wanted and create 360-degree abundance, transforming every area of my life—mind, body, spirit, relationships, finances, and business. I made a commitment to myself to no longer be broken. I decided that no matter what season of life I was in, I would thrive, not merely survive. This book shares my journey from brokenness to abundance.

Want to know how I did it? Keep reading, and I'll share the good, the bad, and the ugly. I won't leave you alone as you evolve from brokenness to 360-degree abundance. The journey is filled with high-high and low-lows, but in the end, I promise you it's all worth it.

Chapter 1
Come with Us, Ma'am

That day should have been another typical Friday. I started my morning around six o'clock, as I always did, with a bowl of oatmeal and honey and lots of praise music, dancing around the house to Mary Mary's "Shackles." I am by no means a singer, but you couldn't tell me anything as I was hitting all my moves in the mirror and using my brush as a microphone. I felt good. It was going to be a great day.

Outside, the sun was shining brightly, and the temperature was perfect—not too cold on that winter day in Georgia. I had to attend a real estate closing, and then I'd do a little grocery shopping to make sure I had food to cook for the weekend. I was starting to eat healthier and was experimenting with different types of foods, including meat substitutes, soy, and organic foods. I made no claims of being a professional chef, but I could hold my own in the kitchen. Let my friends tell it, and I should have had my own cooking show on Food Network. *Cooking with T. Reneé* actually had a nice ring to it.

On the way to the closing, traffic was surprisingly light for morning rush hour, so I arrived early to the attorney's office. The receptionist, a tall blonde dressed in a pretty navy-blue pants suit, greeted me with a great big smile and escorted me to a stately conference room with double mahogany doors and a rectangular glass table. I had waited about ten minutes, when a six-foot-tall attorney with an athletic build and the face of a magazine model walked in with a folder filled with closing documents.

We were reviewing the items in the folder, a process I'd gone through before, when the conference room doors slammed open with a bang. I jumped in my seat and swung around to see what had happened. Ten men—tall, short, Black, and white—and one woman, poured through the door. They wore dark blue vests with FBI written in gold letters across the chest, and before I could get any words out of my mouth, one of them asked me to verify who I was. When I told him my name, he said, "You're under arrest."

I heard the words the agent said, but I didn't fully comprehend them. *Wait a minute. Did he just say I was under arrest? What is happening? Arrested? Me? This can't be!* While the agent continued, listing the charges and reading me my rights, my mind raced with all kinds of thoughts. *Did something happen with one of my businesses? Did I somehow miss that I owed more taxes? What did my business partner do? Did my ex-boyfriend set me up? Has someone stolen my identity? This can't be happening! Maybe the officers have made a mistake. Are they looking for somebody else?*

A female agent and a male agent took me into another room and started to question me. They were polite, but they weren't playing games with me. They took turns drilling me, and they made it clear that they wanted answers to their questions. My own questions continued to swirl in my head until the female agent yelled my name to snap me back into reality.

Once I regained my composure, the two FBI agents resumed their bombardment. What happened on this date? Who is this person? Were you involved in a conspiracy to commit bank fraud? How long have you lived at this address? The interrogation went on for what seemed like days, but may have only been an hour.

Finally, the female officer asked me to stand and put my hands behind my back. Then, she clamped handcuffs on my wrists. I had never been in handcuffs before that moment—not unless you count that one exception that doesn't need mentioning here. This experience was all so surreal. I had on my favorite tailored Dolce & Gabbana bright yellow-gold pantsuit. But my statement accessory wasn't a necklace, a clutch purse, or a handbag. It was a pair of bright silver handcuffs.

The female officer escorted me to the back of the squad car parked right next to my platinum Mercedes-Benz S600. As she did, I ducked my head down and stepped my black Jimmy Choo stiletto boots in the car. The agents seized everything I had in my possession: $15,000 cash for the real estate transaction, my laptop and brown Louis Vuitton briefcase, and my black Gucci purse. They towed away my Mercedes-Benz as I watched. Doggone it! I had just gotten the car washed the day before, and now a muddy tow truck was dragging it away right before my eyes.

As I rode in the back seat of the squad car, I wasn't really sure where jail was or why they were taking me there. Still dazed from the barrage of questions the agents had fired at me one right after the other, I was in a state of shock, denial, and overwhelm. Of course, they'd read me my Miranda rights and told me why I was going to jail, but try as I might, I couldn't comprehend what they told me. I'd heard of people having out-of-body experiences, but it would take me some time to look back and realize what happened to me in that moment. In essence, I was physically present, but my mind had wandered to a place far different from my current reality. Perhaps this was my subconscious mind's way of protecting me from a harsh truth it had seen coming but had failed to prevent from happening.

The two officers driving me, white men in their mid to late forties, chatted with me and tried to make the ride as pleasant as possible. They reminded me of schoolteachers or principals. Contrary to what I would have expected—if I'd ever imagined myself in such a situation—they displayed caring and warm demeanors. Neither of them tried to use his authority to intimidate me, which in the moment, wouldn't have been hard to do.

Their squad car was very clean, and one officer even took the handcuffs off me during the ride. They told me they were taking me to the courthouse to be booked, and since it was

Friday afternoon, I would likely not make bail. I could expect to spend the weekend in the Atlanta Detention Facility. Jail. A place I never thought I'd see the inside of in this lifetime. It was one week before Thanksgiving, and my holiday preparation plans hadn't included an orange jump suit, thick white socks, flip-flop shoes, and group showers.

As I processed all this information, I couldn't help but wonder how my life ended up here. Sure, I'd made some mistakes and bad decisions along the way, but so had everyone else. At just thirty years old, I thought I was living the American dream. I'd been an honor student in high school, graduated from college in three years, worked hard, bought a house, stayed faithful in my relationship, attended church, and helped other people whenever I saw an opportunity to do so. I was a good girl in so many of the ways my parents, teachers, and church leaders had taught me to be, so it made no sense that I found myself headed to jail. Good girl or not, one bad decision was going to cost me my freedom.

*If you live for people's acceptance,
you will die from their rejection.*

LECRAE

Chapter 2
People Pleaser

I'd finally made it. After twelve years of schooling, it was time for me to graduate high school, and I wanted to attend Spelman College or Hampton University. My parents, however, felt like I should stay close to home and go to Georgia State University because of the diversity. We had countless arguments about what they felt was best for me. "We want to expose you to the best education possible to prepare you for the real world," my mother said. "Georgia State," added my father, "is ranked as one of the best business schools in the country, and it's right here in your own backyard. This is a great opportunity for you."

I resisted their logic because I wanted something I couldn't get at Georgia State. I wanted the Black college experience. I had visited my godsister at Hampton University, and I loved the energy on that campus, and I'd gone to summer camp at Spelman College and enjoyed every minute of it. Although I'd attended predominantly Black schools all my life, my experience as a Congressional page had thrust me into a nearly all-white world. As one of three Black pages during my tenure, the culture shock had hit me hard, but it had also nurtured in me an ability to easily navigate situations where everyone didn't look like me. Now my parents wanted me to go to Georgia State for more of the same—and I didn't want to.

"I can get a great education at any of these schools," I told them. "But I want to spread my wings and fly. I want a taste of freedom and independence without a curfew. I want to go to an HBCU to experience campus life, including pledging Delta Sigma Theta Sorority." In essence, I was trying to say, "I want to live my own life, on my own terms, doing what I want to do. I'm eighteen years old, and I want to break free from your control and enjoy the kind of social life I can only find at a historically Black college or university."

Like many parents of their generation, my mother and father believed they knew what was best for me, and in many ways, they did. In this case, they didn't see a reason to hear me out. They were older and wiser, and they had decided. "Does all of that freedom also include you paying for your education, books, room and board, and every other expense you might encounter?" my father asked. My parents ran a very tight ship, and after many conversations like this, I accepted that since they were paying for my schooling, my dreams of pursuing what I really wanted for my college experience were shattered.

While I wanted to do higher education my way, it never occurred to me that I could manage it on my own. I never applied for scholarships, even though I had a 3.7 grade point average and could have qualified for merit awards. I doubted my ability to win enough funds because my SAT scores were a little shaky. After taking the test three or four times, my combined score may have been 900, and most colleges wanted 1,000 or above. In retrospect, I could have pulled it off and won scholarships to attend a college or university of my choice. I could have worked to make up the difference. But instead, I let my vision for college life slip away. When it came down to it, I just didn't have the guts to buck my parents and take sole responsibility for my success or my failure.

I never felt like going after what I wanted was an option. If my parents wanted something for me, I thought I should do it, so I followed their plan for me. I attended Georgia State University, where there were no dormitories at the time, and so I continued to live at home instead of having a campus-life experience.

I settled in as a student, did well in school, had an active social life. I even pledged Delta Sigma Theta to become a red-and-white girl. All in all, I had a great experience, but since I was living under my parents' roof, I played it safe and didn't venture outside the lines. I missed out on a lot by not living on campus or in an apartment with a roommate. I was definitely on the straight and narrow, but I yearned for more freedom. I just had no idea how to get it.

● ○ ●

My parents always advised me to never rent an apartment, but to save to buy a house instead, and I followed their advice. In addition, I graduated with absolutely no student loan debt. Looking from the outside in, I had nothing to complain about. Most people my age would have loved to walk into their adult life with no student debt and a four-year degree from a prestigious college.

Although I majored in business, my dream was never to become a corporate executive. Instead, I felt called to become a motivational speaker and life coach to help women live their best life. From as early as the age of five, I stood in the mirror, talking and imagining myself on stage, where I would speak to and motivate an audience of thousands of people. When asked, I always said I wanted to grow up to be a female version of Zig Ziglar, Les Brown, or Tony Robbins. During my early years, few women had reached their level in the field of motivational speaking, so I didn't have that example, but I always gravitated to high-energy leaders who spoke positivity into people's lives. By middle school, I had Oprah on television, but that was about it.

As a teenager and young woman, I imagined myself gracing the stage of Harpo Studios for my appearance on *The Oprah Winfrey Show*. Later, I saw myself sitting in a chair across from Oprah Winfrey under the trees on *Super Soul Sunday* or in the high-back chair on an episode of *Oprah's Lifeclass*. Oprah created an empire by helping women go after and achieve their best lives, and I always felt, deep in my spirit, that my purpose was similar. I didn't have her media empire, but I felt called to help women create abundance in their marriage, in their family, and in their relationship with themselves, regardless of their upbringing or the cards life had dealt them. Even though my life didn't yet look like what I wanted, I had a burning passion for this calling, and deep down, I wanted to pursue it.

My parents, on the other hand, grew up having to earn and work hard for everything they ever received. Their parents provided them with a lot of love, but my parents didn't have many material possessions when they were young, so they stuck to the conventional path of "get a job and save your money." Although in later years they started a business, my parents always saw financial stability as the primary goal of a career. You do what you have to do, they taught me, until you position yourself to do what you love to do.

My father started working at fourteen and helped to financially provide for his own needs. I didn't have to do that. My parents had given me a leg up to build a great life, but they had a clear picture of what that great life should look like. You know: a house with a picket fence, a dog, and 2.5 kids, thirty years working for one company, the gold watch, and retirement. There was only one problem. My parents so wanted this life for me that they forgot to ask me if this was the life I wanted for myself.

I applaud my parents for their effort and dedication. They provided me with a stable and loving childhood. They were wonderful parents, and I was blessed to grow up with them. They poured so much into me and gave me a great foundation for my life. We took family vacations, and I was involved in everything I wanted to do, from dance and drill team to being the first page, in Washington, DC, for civil rights icon Congressman John Lewis. I was the Student Government Association president and president of various other clubs.

I was in the magnet program and took several honors courses. My daily routine was structured, and I was rarely, if ever, at home without one of my parents there with me. I went to school, then piano or dance, and home to do homework. I had very little free time to explore and get in trouble. I did try to sneak out of the house a few times, but with those attempts, I met the wrath of my mother. My parents shielded me from drugs, teenage pregnancy, and most of the peer-pressure related issues many teenagers were exposed to when I was growing up.

Mostly, my girlfriends would hang out with me and spend the night at my house because my mother rarely allowed me to stay in other people's homes. As a mother, I now under-stand why she made that choice, and as restricted as my movements were, I did have fun growing up. I went to dances, prom, the movies, and other social events. It was all very much monitored by my parents and strategically planned by them, but I made the most of it.

My life was one of comfort and stability. I had a wardrobe full of clothes. I had a car to drive at sixteen and never had to worry about paying for gas or insurance. It was never a ques-tion of whether I would go to college; it was just a matter of where.

Starting as early as elementary school, however, I struggled to claim some sense of independence. By second grade, I wanted to pick out my clothes for school, but my mother, for her own reasons, preferred to make those kinds of choices for me. Perhaps she wanted to protect me from making decisions that could harm me in some way. Perhaps she believed controlling every variable of my life would protect me, but to me, it felt like what I wanted didn't count. As I got older, I had a sassy mouth with my mom at times and wanted to do what I wanted, but my parents kept me in line. I was looking for freedom. I wanted my voice to be heard and my opinions to be respected and seen as valid, and when those things didn't happen, I became rebellious for a time.

All in all, I had a very good childhood, and by many standards, I grew up privileged. Although, on the surface, my childhood was great, there were a few cracks in the foundation. Because my parents sheltered me so, I entered adulthood naïve, too trusting, and in many ways, downright gullible. Now, don't get it twisted. That's who I used to be, but that girl is long gone and no longer lives here. Don't try to step to me that way today, or you'll get a rude awakening. (I'm just saying.)

Even as a young adult, I believed one of my responsibilities as a daughter was to please my parents, and that desire to please people carried over into my other relationships, my businesses, and most every area of my life. My parents didn't intentionally raise me to think or behave that way. They just wanted to steer me in the right direction to give me the highest chance to achieve success as they defined it. However, I internalized their messages and processed them to look like people pleasing.

Since I was so used to my parents making decisions for me, it was easy and natural for me to be passive and go along with the decisions other people made for my life. I preferred not to rock the boat, even if it meant doing things I didn't want to do. I despised confrontation, arguments, or having any-body I loved or cared about get mad at me. I struggled to stand up for myself, since I feared repercussions if someone didn't agree with what I said or did. When I graduated college, I had new knowledge and new skills, but I had yet to develop the confidence in my own ability to decide what I truly wanted out of life or the courage and tenacity to go out and get it. I didn't know my own worth, so I allowed others to define it for me.

● ◦ ●

Growing up I was surrounded by dysfunctional relationships in my extended family and in the lives of my friends. Since I had seen it so much, I thought some of this was normal behavior. In one such case, one of my family members left his wife of more than fifteen years and married his mistress. Everyone acted like nothing had happened and immediately embraced the new wife and welcomed her into the family. They invited her to some family events and invited his ex-wife to others. The whole situation struck me as strange, even at a young age, but nobody talked about it. It was the elephant in the room that everybody walked around, stepping over the mess it left behind.

I also observed passive men who allowed their wives to speak to them with total disrespect and run their household any way they wanted. At least, that was how it appeared to me, and it would be years before I had the maturity and experience to realize much of what I saw was just the public face of those relationships. In some cases, the dynamic between husband and wife was quite different than what I had taken it to be. As a child and as an adolescent, however, my mind processed all this dysfunction as normal, and it carried into my future relationships.

I took on the role of the passive one and often allowed men in my life to speak to me any kind of way. In my world, that behavior was normal. Over time, I would learn how to rid myself of being a people pleaser, validate myself, and stop looking to others to approve of and validate me. I would stop depending on other people for feedback and advice and learn to sit with myself and God and not only listen to what He had to say, but also trust myself enough to act on it.

Those changes, however, wouldn't happen for several years—and only after my passivity caused me to make poor choices that significantly impacted my life. I spent years, even decades, pleasing my parents, a man, clients, and everyone else in my life to the detriment of my health, my freedom, and my sanity. I have since learned how to forgive myself, step into my fears instead of running away from them, and go after what I truly want in my life.

It is a daily process. Sometimes I succeed, and other times I fail. However, I have learned to embrace failure as a part of life and have redefined what it means to fail. In my life, F.A.I.L. now means First Attempt In Learning. If my first attempt doesn't work out, I'll just try a second, third, or fourth time, or however many times it takes, to get the result I want. I've learned how to take it easy on myself and not put so much pressure on myself.

I can be my harshest critic, and some days I just need to love on myself without criticism and judgment. I fully embrace that where I am in life is exactly where I am supposed to be. I have transformed from a people pleaser to a God pleaser, which has made life way more enjoyable, purposeful, and peaceful. I've lost some friends along the way, but I understand that's sometimes part of the process.

Given those changes and who I am today, many people who know me find it hard to believe I was once so focused on pleasing other people that I tolerated a "romantic" relationship that can only be described as abusive, but that's what I stepped into as I tried to find a way to live life on my own terms.

When someone shows you
who they are, believe them the
first time.

MAYA ANGELOU

Chapter 3
Things Aren't Always as They Appear

One Friday evening in 1994, my second year of college, my godsister called me and asked if I wanted to go out, and we decided to go dancing. I put on a cute little floral-print dress with heels, and we headed out to a club. I was feeling single and ready to mingle. Still underage, this was my first time going to a real club, but fake ID in hand, I was ready.

A few minutes after we stepped into the club, a very handsome young man caught my eye. He was wearing a blue button-down shirt, jeans, and black dress shoes. His hair was wavy and cut low, his face cleanly shaven. I must have caught his eye too because, not long into the night, I felt a tap on my shoulder, and our eyes connected as he asked me to dance. This guy had some moves. We danced to popular music by Janet Jackson, Jodeci, Xscape, and whoever else was climbing the R&B charts. He introduced himself as Kent, and we talked the whole night.

Kent and I exchanged numbers, and to my delight, he called me the next day. We talked for three hours. He lived in Florida and was only in town for one more day, so we decided to get together. Our first date was a lot of fun. We went to Houston's restaurant in Buckhead, an upscale Atlanta neighborhood, and enjoyed a great conversation. I had a grilled chicken salad with vinaigrette dressing, and he had grilled salmon with a baked potato and salad. We laughed and shared a lot. Kent told me he had never been married, didn't have any kids, and worked in sales and training for a telecommunications company. It's funny how I remember all those details, but some moments are so pivotal, they're hard to forget.

He thought I was older because we'd met in a club, and I thought he was younger, closer to my age. I was nineteen at the time, and it turned out he was twenty-six. He was definitely the oldest guy I had dated, but I was open and didn't see it as a problem. In fact, the idea of an older man with more life experience pursuing me intrigued me and made me feel special. I felt like a giddy schoolgirl, and I was instantly smitten with him. Kent charmed me with all the right words and more intense attention than I'd ever gotten from a man.

Our relationship went from zero to one hundred in a matter of a few months. In the beginning, he sent me dozens of roses at my parents' house and at the office where I held an internship. He frequently drove up to Atlanta to visit me, and I visited him in Florida a couple of times, telling my parents I had some event or another for my internship. We dined at five-star restaurants, and we shopped at stores I could barely pronounce the names of, like Ermenegildo Zegna, Diane von Furstenberg, and Bulgari. For a young girl who had seen very little of the world, this was all captivating. This was the kind of courtship I'd read about in novels and seen in movies. It felt like so much more than anything the people in my life had experienced, and enjoying such an exceptional experience made me feel special.

While I was caught up in my new romance, my parents weren't very fond of Kent. From the beginning, my dad suspected Kent was trying to buy my love. When he sent four dozen roses to me, at my parents' house, for our four-month anniversary, the gesture thrilled me, but it only served to reinforce my father's opinion. My mother didn't verbalize her opinion to me very much, but even in her near silence, it was clear she agreed with my father.

Regardless of my parents' position, I felt like I had hit the jackpot. I was head over heels in love, or so I thought. I had met a man who I felt truly loved and supported me, and my nose was wide open. About nine months after we started dating, Kent moved to Atlanta. He helped me study, and while I was still in school and interning with AT&T, we launched our first business together. Kent encouraged me to graduate from college in just three years. He even threw me a lavish twenty-first birthday party and invited all my friends and family to celebrate with us in a hotel ballroom filled with balloons and a huge cake. It was so thoughtful of him, and I had a great time.

One night, when we were looking at cars in a closed car lot, Kent stopped, and there in the middle of the sedans and SUVs and sports cars, he got down on one knee, pulled out a diamond ring, and proposed to me. We'd been dating just over a year.

"Boy, get up and stop playing," I said, laughing.

The look on his face let me know he was very serious, but he quickly put the ring back in his pocket. When I tried to discuss it, Kent wouldn't talk about the surprise proposal, and he never brought it up again. I truly loved him, but I was way too young to get married, and I knew my parents would have a fit. They didn't care for Kent as my boyfriend, and they definitely didn't approve of him as my choice for a husband.

On the surface, all was great. However, when you peeled back some of the layers, things weren't as they appeared. At one point, Kent, who always portrayed himself as doing well financially, hit a rough patch—so rough that he no longer had a car to drive. In an effort to be a supportive girlfriend, I loaned him my new car, the first I'd ever purchased for myself. Every day, he'd drop me off at work and then drive off for the day. When my parents found out about our temporary arrangement, they expressed their unhappiness, but I was an adult, and they couldn't choose who I dated.

Eventually, I found out Kent's financial issues ran even deeper. When we first met, he'd told me he had never been married and didn't have any children. A few years later, there was a knock at his door while we were watching a movie. "County sheriff," a voice called out. We opened the door, and lo and behold, the sheriff announced he had come to arrest Kent for back child support.

Back child support? For what child?

As the sheriff whisked him away, there wasn't any time for questions, but that didn't stop me from yelling, "What the hell is going on?" Normally, I don't curse, but I believed this situation warranted it. Kent responded, "Call an attorney."

A few hours later, he called and asked me to look on top of the refrigerator, in the very back, and open a manila envelope hidden there. I felt like an investigator digging for paperwork or looking for clues. To my surprise, divorce papers with a proposed child support decree were in the envelope.

Reading through the papers, I was totally confused. We had been together for almost four years, and this was the first time I'd ever heard about a wife and kids. In fact, he had clearly told me, when we first started dating, that he'd never been married or had kids. I had a long list of questions, but rather than ask them while he was on a detention center phone, I conferenced his mother into the call. When Kent told her what had happened, she said, "I had a feeling your wife never filed the divorce papers." Apparently, Kent and his wife had been separated for almost five years and had two children together, girls seven and nine years old.

I found myself involved in one tangled web. My first thought should have been: *This man has lied to you for almost four years. Run for your life.* But it wasn't. Instead, I wanted to get it all straightened out. This was my first serious relationship, and I believed this was what love looked like. When you ran into a problem, you worked it out. Even though we weren't married or even engaged, I was fully committed, and to me that meant helping him through, around, or over every obstacle he faced. I'd also stepped fully into the peacemaker role, a role I'd watched my father occupy in our family for years, but in my case, it meant dismissing red flags and blatant offenses for the sake of staying together.

Kent was smooth, charismatic, and always knew exactly what to say. He gave me a detailed sob story about how the mother of his children—his wife—had an affair, left him, and was making it difficult for him to see his kids. Of course, he was the victim. I tell you this was an Oscar nomination in the making. I can make light of it now, but it was no laughing matter back then. I rallied the troops: a good attorney and a court-ordered child support and parenting plan. I thought, *if you have children, you need to be heavily involved in their lives, and I am here to support you, one hundred percent.*

● ● ●

Once the divorce was final, Kent and I had the kids for the summer. Always the overachiever, I went into overdrive—tennis lessons, swimming at the pool, trips to Six Flags, movies, shopping, and all the fun stuff kids like to do. I wanted to provide them with the best summer experience they'd ever had. I was so conscious of our influence on their little minds that I even slept downstairs in the basement or went to my parents' house so the children wouldn't see me shacking with their dad. (Sorry, Mom.)

In fact, if I stayed overnight with Kent and the kids, I slept on the floor because there wasn't a bed in our basement. I can only imagine what Kent thought when he saw I was not only willing to stay with him and support him after all his lies, but I was also willing to sleep on the floor. Those choices only served to reinforce the lopsided power dynamic in our relationship.

The summer went so well that the kids went back home bragging to their mom about how much fun they had with us. (I'll leave it to your imagination to figure out how well that went over with their mother.) Because the kids were content, Kent was happy, and I felt like I had accomplished my goal. I fooled myself into thinking we had it all figured out because anything less would mean I'd invested all my time and energy into a man who wasn't for me and a relationship that would never work. I wasn't ready to face that possibility.

Trust is like paper. Once it's crumbled, it can't be perfect again.

AUTHOR UNKNOWN

Chapter 4
And Still Counting

Two years after I found out about Kent's two daughters, everything appeared to be on track on the family front. We regularly had his daughters with us, and he was reestablishing his bond with them. Life was going pretty well—until I got hit with another curve ball.

One Saturday morning, we were discussing our plans for the day when Kent told me his brother had run into an old friend. I tried to decipher the words coming out of his mouth as the conversation continued. It sounded like he said this old friend was actually baby momma number two and his two children had now expanded to three children, but of course, that couldn't be the case. I listened as he went on with this revelation.

Once I decoded the information, I realized that before he was married, when he was in his late teens or early twenties, he'd fathered a child with a woman he'd dated off and on for years. Apparently, shortly after the child was born, they broke up, and from the time of her birth, he was in and out of his daughter's life. While Kent didn't show up for his firstborn as much as he should have, his parents kept in touch with their granddaughter and spent quite a bit of time with her.

This was more than a red flag. This new information was a huge "LEAVE NOW" signpost. He had lied to me from our very first date, and continued to lie, only revealing the truth, a little at a time, when faced with undeniable evidence. He had watched me play with and take care of his younger two children, and he'd still kept his older child a secret. His duplicity made me wonder what else he might be lying about, but I pushed those thoughts away. And I stayed.

Kent and the child's mother began to talk, and he slowly established a relationship with his oldest daughter. It appeared, however, that as his relationship with his daughter grew, his relationship with her mother also found new life. They shared late night phone calls and lots of family outings that didn't include me. In fact, Kent never even introduced me to this child's mother. I was naïve, but I wasn't stupid, and I questioned him about it.

Kent went off. "I thought you wanted to support me in this. I'm trying to get to know my daughter!" After accusing me of not being supportive enough, he assured me his only focus was to be there for his daughter and nothing else. "This is a process," he told me more than once, explaining that it would take time to ensure his daughter felt completely comfortable spending time alone with him, without her mother present, since he and his daughter had been apart for so long.

In the midst of all of this drama, I had a conversation with his parents during a weekend trip to his hometown. We talked about everything going on with Kent, and then they dropped a bomb. His parents disclosed to me that the boy they were raising (who I always believed was a family friend's child) might also be Kent's. Now, he had three children and a possible—all of whose existence he'd lied to me about. I know it sounds like a Spades game, but this was real life here.

When Kent and I talked about the possible fourth child, he insisted it wasn't true, but his parents clearly thought otherwise. Kent went from zero children to two, then three, and finally, possibly four. I didn't think that was what God had in mind when He said multiply and fill the earth.

As I write this story, I'm shaking my head and feeling very sorry for that young woman who was me many years ago. What in the world was I thinking? Three or four children I had no idea about, lies, deception, and betrayal, and I was still there. When I first met this man, I was so young and naïve. Kent was my first real boyfriend. He was accomplished, smart, romantic, and thoughtful. The first few years of our relationship seemed magical, and I was all in. I was that "ride or die" kind of chick for him. (People who know me are laughing as they read this because they can't imagine me talking like that.)

I gave him everything—my trust, my heart, and my loyalty—and he took a lot—my confidence, my self-esteem, and my self-worth. I guess I shouldn't say he took it. In truth, I allowed him to have it because I didn't know who I really was or how to recognize my own value.

Our relationship alienated me from my friends and family. As I was separated more and more from my larger support network, Kent became my go-to person for everything in business, family, and life. His voice became the only voice influencing me, and sadly, his voice spoke to me much more loudly than my own. He became jealous, controlling, and manipulative as our relationship went on, but I confused that behavior with him being protective and loving. He could be mentally, verbally, and emotionally abusive, yet he could also be very loving and caring. Most of the time, I walked around on eggshells because I wasn't sure what would set him off. I wasn't confrontational. In fact, I continued to be the peacekeeper, like my father, and at the time, I preferred to keep quiet rather than have an argument I could only lose. Kent was always right and never apologized for anything, even when the evidence was stacked against him.

Whatever Kent wanted from me, he got. I was afraid to lose him, and I did everything, right or wrong, I could do to please him. In one case that fell on the "wrong" side of the spectrum, I allowed him to negatively influence me into a choice that would have huge repercussions on my life for years to come.

Money was getting low in our business, and we had used up all our personal credit, so Kent suggested we get a business loan. We did all the research and prepared our business loan package, including projections, financial information, and a business plan, but loan officers were unimpressed. After receiving refusal after refusal from various banks because we didn't have a huge list of clients or collateral to back the loan,

Kent had this bright idea that we should inflate the financial numbers and embellish our client list.

I was so used to blindly doing what he asked or told me to do that I never took the time to sit back and really assess what he was suggesting. He assured me the goal was to use the money to build our business. "We're not hurting anybody," he said. "We'll pay back the loan as soon as these contracts we're working on close." Obedient, I didn't question him.

We received the first loan, and Kent grew more arrogant and careless with spending. It was like he had proven to himself that he could do whatever he wanted. He also became more jealous and domineering. Our relationship was in a bad place. He would often tell me he made me into who I was and nobody else would want me, and I believed him. After all, in many ways, I had allowed him to mold me into someone I otherwise wouldn't have become. In fact, I had molded myself to his specifications. I don't know exactly when our relationship shifted to this dynamic—the process was gradual—but it did.

Later, a counselor told me a powerful thing. She said when women are in abusive relationships of any type, the relationships typically don't start off with abuse. It's like putting a frog in cold water and slowly turning up the temperature. By the time the water is scalding hot, the frog is used to it because the change has happened slowly. Even as my controlling boyfriend turned up the heat on me, I continued to put aside my dreams of speaking from stages and uplifting women so I could build his business dreams.

Success is not about what you have but who you become.

_____

T. RENEÉ SMITH

Chapter 5
Building an Empire

Throughout our ten-year relationship, Kent and I built several businesses together. Some of them achieved great success, others not so much. We had very humble beginnings in business, including days when we slept in our tiny office space because we had gotten evicted from our condo. During those tough times, I took bird baths in the office breakroom sink. I bought a bucket to stand in, and I let water run down into it as I performed my hygiene routine each day. Living like I was homeless was so ridiculous because I could have easily gone back home to my parents. But again, I was that "ride or die" chick. I was going to be there to the end to support my man.

At one of our financial low points, I even cleaned out my childhood piggy bank. It was funny because I thought I'd find several hundred dollars in there because I'd been saving coins since I was three years old. It turned out to be $55.83, but when your pockets are empty, that's a lot of money. We used it to buy Happy Meals and other inexpensive food items.

We also hid our cars so they wouldn't get repossessed. At this time, we had several contracts pending in the pipeline; they just weren't closing fast enough. We were doing everything we could just to make ends meet and stay above water.

Initially, we started off working hard together to build our businesses. The first venture was a telecommunications company, followed by a website design firm, and eventually a record label. Yes, we schmoozed with some of the biggest entertainers, and we were in recording studios with some of the hottest talent. We attended the Grammys and had a ball producing music videos, hosting concerts, and learning the business. I enjoyed every bit of the glamour, the access, and the special treatment, but my energy came from quiet time and time spent at home. I began to recognize I was really more of an introvert and just as satisfied with behind-the-scenes work as I was with being in the spotlight.

From sunup to sundown, work filled my days. I was young and didn't have kids of my own yet, so my sole purpose was to grind and build a successful business. Even though none of these businesses fulfilled my dreams or my passion, I knew a lot of sweat equity was required to make them successful. I kept at it because I wanted to support my man.

Whatever venture we took on, I was all in, every time. I took time to really learn each industry and studied successful companies and the strategies they used to make it to the top. I was patient and understood anything worth having was going to require lots and lots of work. Kent, on the other hand, liked really big results, really fast. He liked to manage, and oversee, and tell others what to do. He wasn't very fond of doing the work and getting his hands dirty, but he loved being the boss.

Kent's motto, "Live lavishly and show off," conflicted with my motto, "Live modestly and be conservative." He was quite materialistic and always wanted to wear the latest fashions and drive the latest cars. I, on the other hand, was fine driving my red Ford Explorer. I really loved that car, but he thought it was bad for the business's image and I needed to drive a Mercedes or a Hummer, so he bought me one of each. I was just fine shopping at Rich's (which later merged with Macy's), but he believed I should only wear designer clothes. He controlled my image and decided exactly what I would wear and how my hair would look. He bought my clothes and selected my hairstylist.

I couldn't admit it then, but our values and priorities weren't in sync at all. I was a bit too simple for him. I wasn't into make-up, and I felt just fine dressed in jeans and a T-shirt. He wanted a specific high-fashion look, including long flowing weaves, for his woman. I got dressed up and played the part, but it really wasn't me. I preferred tennis shoes, on any day, to heels and a natural hairdo to weave and acrylic nails.

Don't get me wrong. I will get some gel nails and put on stilettos and a cute dress when I'm feeling myself and want to show up as feminine and stylish, but that is not my everyday normal. For Kent, I pretended like it was. I went along with his program and put my all into whatever business idea appealed to him in the moment, and before long, we reached heights most entrepreneurs only dream of reaching.

*People who shine from within
don't need the spotlight.*

AUTHOR UNKNOWN

Chapter 6
In the Limelight

Our business had us traveling back and forth from the East Coast to the West Coast on a regular basis. During one of our trips to Los Angeles, California, we decided to just chill for a little bit and see the city, and we ended up going to a tattoo parlor. I was talking to the owner and looking at different designs when Kent interrupted with a question. "Have you ever thought about getting my name tattooed on you?" he asked. I said I hadn't, and he responded, "Since we're going to be together and you love me, I think you should." My response was still no.

Now, I might have put up with some insane stuff in our relationship, but my momma didn't raise a fool. I had no intention of getting his name permanently inked on my body. Given where our relationship was at the time, no reasonable person would've even asked me that, but you would have thought I'd called his mother every kind of whore with the way he responded to the word *no* coming out of my mouth. This two-letter word enraged him.

Kent's demeanor totally switched, and in that moment, I had no idea who he was. I had seen a few different sides of him come out, but this one was new to me. He went from cursing me out, to accusing me of cheating on him, to calling me everything but a child of God.

I stood there looking at him as he ranted. All the while I thought: *Are you coo-coo for coco puffs? You have four children who I didn't know about (well, three confirmed), you are probably cheating on me (I don't have proof, but I do have a woman's intuition), you are jealous and treat me like your property, and you want me to put your name on my body? You have lost your mind.*

Maybe he could sense my thoughts or maybe he ran out of steam. Either way, he finally ended his tirade and ordered me to get in the car. Back at the hotel, he told me to pack my bags. Then he rushed me to the airport and put me on the next plane to Atlanta, while he stayed in California.

● ● ●

On the surface, Kent and I recovered from the tattoo fiasco, but it left another crack in the already crumbling foundation of our relationship. After the L.A. trip, I started spending more time at my parents' house to give our relationship some space. It was the only way I could find room to breathe since he and I lived and worked together. In the following weeks, I spent more and more time with my parents, until for all practical purposes, I was living at home once again.

On the business front, life was moving really fast. One day, we were living in an apartment, launching a business from home, and just a few short years later, we were in a 10,000-square-foot office, and I was being featured in *Cosmopolitan* and *Entrepreneur* magazines. It was an amazing ride. Because of my new level of visibility, congratulations for my achievements poured in from all over. A few potential suitors even sent me flowers at the office because the articles never mentioned if I was married, involved, or single. I was flattered, but Kent wasn't.

One day, a large bouquet of red roses arrived with a card from a man I'd never met. Kent didn't bother to ask me what my relationship was to this man or if I even knew him. Instead, he gave me such a harsh tongue-lashing about being disrespectful and ungrateful that I didn't know if I was coming or going. The attention I was getting enraged him because, as far as he was concerned, it was his idea and his business. I never asked for any of it, and being in the limelight made me a bit uncomfortable, but I continued because the publicity was good for the business.

As I received more accolades, Kent started to criticize everything I did. He constantly reminded me that if it weren't for him, none of this would have happened. He traveled more, spent more, and questioned my loyalty more. His mood swings became unbearable. He was angry more than he was happy, and he seemed to always have something negative to say.

He didn't seem to understand I would have gladly given up worrying about what I wore because people recognized me on airplanes and in stores. I wanted a business that created financial freedom for me, but fame, even on a small level, felt more like a burden than a perk.

Under the stress of his fragile ego and his constant bad temper, our relationship became strained. He stopped answering his phone in front of me and started taking most of his business trips by himself. Kent accused me of cheating on him and had problems with me working with male clients. He found fault in nearly everything I did.

One day, Kent complained that he was feeling sick, so I brought him some soup and medicine. However, I didn't call before I came over. I rang the doorbell, but he came out of the garage instead of answering the front door. "Oh, thank you, baby, so much," he said, "but I'm really not feeling well and just want to rest."

My female antenna immediately went up. *You just want to rest, huh? And you didn't open the front door?* After that incident, I paid closer attention, and I noticed a lot of other suspicious things. For instance, when he was in New York on business, he called me to check in, but his phone didn't hang up properly when we were done, and I heard a female voice in the background. I listened for a while, but all I heard was general conversation. Another time, he called me when he was out of town, visiting his parents. I missed his call, and it went to voicemail, but when I called him back, a woman answered his phone. He told me she was his cousin, and I had no way to prove otherwise.

By that point, we'd been together for almost a decade, practically my entire adult life. I was so drained and exhausted from our relationship. Something had to change. I didn't know how to escape because we'd built a life in which all things business and personal were intertwined, but I was miserable. I had completely lost myself. I didn't know who I was or what I really wanted in life. I felt stuck. While I wanted to flee, I froze between fear of leaving him and fear of staying with him. I was so confused and needed help.

Looking for answers, I started going to church and praying, reaching out to God. On more than one night, as I lay in my bed, I prayed, "God, I know you have more for me in my life. You want me to be happy, and I am not. I don't feel like I can do anything right. Please change my relationship and my life." I also sought spiritual guidance from a family friend and reconnected with my girlfriends, who spoke some much-needed reality into my life.

As our relationship spiraled out of control, so did our business. Our financial commitments became overwhelming, the business loans were reaching maturity, and our revenues were drying up. We were spending way more money than the business was making, all in an effort to create the image he wanted the world to see. Kent needed to wear the latest designer clothes, fly first class, take expensive vacations, and dine in five-star restaurants, and I'd gone along with all of it.

We spent most of our revenues on liabilities, not assets, and we invested little money back into the business to help it grow.

The same day my issue of *Cosmopolitan* came out, we were served notice for a lawsuit resulting from unpaid bills and a notice of eviction from our office space for past due rent. Everything went haywire at the same time. And it would get worse before it got better.

Maturity is learning to walk away from people and situations that threaten your peace of mind, self-respect, values, morals, or self-worth.

AUTHOR UNKNOWN

Chapter 7
The Fairy Tale Is Over

Looking in from the outside, most people thought I was living a fabulous life: expensive cars, a beautiful house, designer clothes, trips to the spa, and meals at five-star restaurants. That life as I knew it was about to change.

I was in a deep sleep when a phone call awakened me at two o'clock in the morning. My mind immediately went to worst-case scenarios because I didn't normally get calls at that time. Little did I know I was about to be dethroned as queen. My supposed fairy tale was about to end.

As soon as I answered, Kent said, "We need to talk." He told me things hadn't been right with us for a while, and we both knew where this was headed. He told me he had been dating someone else for some time. Four months earlier, he said, they had gotten married, and now his new wife was expecting. He explained that he didn't want to be by himself, so he got married before he broke up with me.

I dropped the phone and struggled to catch my breath so I wouldn't hyperventilate. My body went numb with disbelief. The man I had been with for over a decade, and with whom I'd just spent the weekend with in New York, had gotten married while still in a relationship with me. I knew we were having problems, of course. I even knew I wanted something different, but I hadn't seen the breakup coming. How could the man I'd built a life with (or so I thought) do this to me?

Even with all our problems, I'd clung to some hope that he would change, that our relationship would return to the affection and excitement we'd once shared, and we'd find our happily ever after. After all we'd gone through together, I believed we'd be heading to the altar soon and starting our own family. Even though I'd declined his proposal years earlier, I always thought in my heart that we would be husband and wife. My loyalty to him had never wavered. I'd invested so much time and effort in him and in us, and I'd convinced myself that investment would pay off sooner or later.

My heart was completely broken. This was, in essence, the only man I'd ever known. Sure, I'd experienced silly little crushes in high school, but nothing of real substance. Kent and I had lived together, off and on, and spent most of our time together since we met. My life had completely revolved around him for so long that I had no idea who I was without him. I had alienated friends and family for our relationship. It had always been him and me, Bonnie and Clyde.

During our relationship, Kent often discouraged me from spending much time with my family or friends. He believed they didn't like him, which in many cases was true, and he wasn't comfortable around them either. Whenever I visited with my family or friends, he called eight, nine, ten times, and I could always expect an argument when I got back to him. I could never enjoy myself when I was with them because the constant pressure of his calls and the debriefing process when I returned were exhausting. I soon learned to decline most invitations to hang out with family or friends. Without coming out and saying I had to choose, Kent gave me an ultimatum, and time after time, I chose him.

During our time together, our seven-year age gap had frequently caused problems in our relationship because he had expectations that I would be more mature than I was. He solved that problem by simply dictating my actions, and by this time, I'd become dependent on him to tell me what to do. Rather than two partners making decisions together, he'd become the authority figure, planning my life for me, but I couldn't see it at the time.

Now, I had to deal with a new reality, and I had no idea what to do. The man I'd built my life with, with whom I'd shared everything, had abandoned me. I had lost my way and the ability to make sound decisions for myself. Allowing someone else to determine my fate would turn out to be my biggest downfall.

When I told my parents Kent and I had broken up, they couldn't hide their joy. They wanted so much more for me, and my dad reminded me he'd never believed Kent was a suitable man for me. From the beginning, he'd watched Kent try to buy my love and use money and things to manipulate me. My mom felt much the same way, and while they were both right, I couldn't bring myself to tell them the whole truth. I couldn't break it to my parents that this man I'd fought so hard to be with had gotten another woman pregnant and married her while I continued to sacrifice for him and for our relationship. By the time they found out, we'd all have bigger worries.

My life started to fall apart. I had alienated much of my family, endured Kent's mental and verbal abuse, and placed my life on hold so he could pursue his dreams. That may sound bad, but it got worse. One would think I would cut my losses, bandage my wounds, and go on my merry way after discovering my man had started a whole new family before he broke up with me. No, not I. Instead, I stuck around, mesmerized by the web I was caught in. While I didn't meet her, I helped him and his new wife as we continued to run the business he and I had started together. For some reason, I couldn't let go.

When Kent and I were together, I was the one who made sure all the bills were paid. I guess he forgot that while he was out spreading his seed and replenishing the earth, and as fate would have it, or as Georgia Power would have it, shortly after he ended our relationship, his electricity was cut off. Even though I stayed enmeshed in his life, I assumed that since we weren't together anymore, he would pay his own bills.

I'd worked with the interior designer and builder for almost two years to design the house he and his new wife now lived in. It was supposed to be for Kent and me and I was crushed when I realized my dream of us raising a family together in that home had died. However, even with everything I'd put into the house, I didn't expect to keep doing the same after we broke up. My name wasn't on the deed for that property or any other house he owned, and while it hurt that my home had been snatched away from me, it also meant it was no longer my responsibility. Kent must have ignored notices from the power company for months. After all, they give you a few months to catch up before they shut off your power.

When a woman receives a phone call from her ex-boyfriend saying he needs help with his electricity bill for the house where he lives with his new wife, she will: a) ignore the call, b) answer the call and cuss him out, or c) answer, cuss him out, and hang up. I chose d) none of the above. I chose to help him.

For four months, the pastor in my church had been teaching on unconditional love. He explained that if you truly love someone unconditionally, you don't treat him the way he treats you. You treat him the way you would want to be treated. My pastor also said that if you have unconditional love for a person, you want him to be happy even if it's not with you.

Apparently, God was giving me a pop quiz on patience, long-suffering, faith, and every other word about love in 1 Corinthians 13:3-10. He was really testing me to see what I was made of, and I wanted to pass with honors.

If I give everything I own to the poor and even go to the stake to be burned as a martyr, but I don't love,

I've gotten nowhere. So, no matter what I say, what I believe, and what I do, I'm bankrupt without love.

Love never gives up.
Love cares more for others than for self.
Love doesn't want what it doesn't have.
Love doesn't strut,
Doesn't have a swelled head,
Doesn't force itself on others,
Isn't always "me first,"
Doesn't fly off the handle,
Doesn't keep score of the sins of others,
Doesn't revel when others grovel,
Takes pleasure in the flowering of truth,
Puts up with anything,
Trusts God always,
Always looks for the best,
Never looks back,
But keeps going to the end.
Love never dies.

1 Corinthians 13:3-10 (MSG)
Copyright © 1993, 2002, 2018 by Eugene H. Peterson

A voice told me to go ahead and pay the entire balance owed for the electric bill, and I'd love to say I immediately obeyed, but I would be lying. First, I said, "God, I know this is not of you. Get behind me, Satan." (Yes, I said those words out loud for God and everyone to hear.) Second, I spoke a few choice words that I care not to repeat on these pages. Finally, I had a conversation with myself over several hours.

I knew in my heart what I had to do. I paid the entire balance. With that, I believed I was finished with the whole ordeal. Then, I heard a voice say I should pray for Kent and his new wife.

Now wait a minute, God, I thought. *You're asking way too much of me. I'm a woman scorned. First, you make me give away my money, and then you want me to pray for someone who has betrayed me and lied to me.*

In response to my complaint, God took me back to Scripture and told me to remember what unconditional love is. If you truly love a person, then it doesn't matter what they have done to you. It matters how you respond.

Let's be honest. The first few, ten, or twenty times I prayed for Kent and his wife, the prayer came from my head, not from my heart. God told me to keep praying until I meant it, and so I did. That day, I prayed for hours upon hours until I reached a point where I truly desired happiness and peace for the two of them in their life together.

Over that time, God showed me those prayers weren't only for the newlyweds. They also served to uproot all the bitterness and unforgiveness I had in my spirit where Kent and his new wife were concerned. God helped me to understand and accept that if the relationship had been meant for me, it would have lasted. It wasn't meant for me, and there was nothing I could do to hold on to it.

I released Kent from my life that day, and I forgave myself for all I had put up with and sacrificed. It was freeing, and it started my healing process. I still had a long way to go, but at least I could do it without the added weight of bitterness and unforgiveness. I had no idea that this forgiveness and love I had in my heart would soon have to sustain me during the biggest trial of my life.

For every action, there is an equal and opposite reaction.

ISAAC NEWTON

Chapter 8
You Are Not Above the Law

A t thirty years old and in the midst of profound heartache, I had forgiven Kent and wanted him to be completely happy, but I knew we could no longer work together. Just a few months after our relationship ended, there were two pressing tasks I needed to handle: first, buy a house of my own, and second, bring closure to our business relationship.

At that time, I still wasn't making the best business or personal decisions. The fact that I had helped my ex-boyfriend build his dream house for his new wife, all the while believing he and I would live together there, made me feel like I deserved my own dream house. I was in no financial or emotional position to be purchasing a home, but I did it anyway.

I worked with the realtor for several months to find the perfect house, and she delivered. It was an eight-thousand-square-foot, three-story, three-car-garage house with a pool, Jacuzzi, and theater room. The owner's suite took up half the upstairs and had two expansive walk-in closets and a personal study. The house could have been torn from the pages of a magazine.

Throughout the process of buying this luxury home, I never stopped to ask myself what in the world I planned to do with six bedrooms, two offices, a piano room, and more space than I could imagine using. I'm a little embarrassed to say it, but the house was so big I was scared to spend the night in it by myself. This purchase was truly an emotional decision. It did not make a bit of sense for me to buy a house so far outside of my budget. I was single with no kids, and I basically used two rooms: my bedroom and the kitchen. Good decision or bad, I was in the house and had to turn my attention to business.

I needed to figure out how to quickly exit the business partnerships Kent and I had started and built together. With an entrepreneur bug that would never go away, I was unemployable, but I was ready to start my own business and run it the right way. I imagined that once I severed our business ties, I'd go on with my life, take the lessons learned, and allow everything we'd gone through to fade into memory. Little did I know that figuring out how to cut our professional ties was the least of my problems.

We still had several outstanding business lines of credit that we owed substantial amounts of money on, and we had to figure out how to pay them off. We had one property with some equity in it, and I decided to take the equity out of that house and use it to pay down some of the business expenses. I went to the attorney's office to sign the paperwork, which should have only taken about thirty minutes. However, the events that took place that day forever changed my life.

The receptionist escorted me to the conference room and told me to have a seat. Within a few minutes, the attorney came in with the HUD statement, and we reviewed it together. As I leaned over the table to read the document, ten FBI agents stormed the room. One of them asked me to verify who I was and told me I was under arrest. A female agent and a male agent took me into a room and started to question me. They were polite, but they definitely drilled me and wanted answers to their questions.

I was physically present, but my mind was somewhere else, trying to process everything going on. I'm sure they told me, but at that point, I didn't hear anyone confirm why I was being arrested. I could only assume the bad loans had finally caught up to us.

Once I really came to, you would think I would've been scared and nervous, but I felt a sense of peace and calm. For so long, I'd felt like I was trapped in somebody else's body, just looking at my life from the outside. I had become numb to the disrespect, lies, verbal abuse, and the cheating I tried not to see. I couldn't put my finger on it at the time, but I had known for a long time before our breakup that something wasn't right. The life we had together was definitely not the life I wanted for myself, but I would always say, "At least I know what I have in this man." I didn't want to go back out and start dating because I might get something worse. After all that, I wasn't angry or mad that I was about to get arrested. Surprisingly enough, I was actually happy.

For so long before I found out about Kent's betrayal, I'd prayed that God would deliver our relationship and make it better. I prayed He would change my ex, which was the wrong prayer. God answered my prayer differently than I ever expected. He changed me and gave me a clear and certain exit out of the relationship and the business. Because my state of mind was so messed up, if I hadn't been provided with forced closure, if Kent hadn't ended things with me, I'd probably still be there today. Come hell or high water, when I put my mind to something, it's going to happen. I had always been very loyal; when we were together, we were together, no matter what. I'm still incredibly loyal today, but I have now defined my boundaries and "no matter what" isn't a part of my thinking anymore. Back then, sticking it out looked like love to me.

After an hour of questioning at the attorney's office, I was taken to a detention facility. It was late on a Friday afternoon, so I wasn't able to appear in front of the judge to make bond. Instead, I spent Friday, Saturday, and Sunday in jail and had a bond hearing scheduled on Monday. Over the weekend, I contacted my brother, and he spoke to my parents on my behalf. They hired an attorney to appear with me at the bond hearing. The only thing I could do was make the best of the weekend.

Along with a group of women in similar circumstances, I walked into the Atlanta Detention Facility in handcuffs. It was very late in the evening, and everyone was getting ready for lights out. I asked the guard for a Bible, went into my cell, and sat on the top bunk. So many thoughts ran through my head.

Lord, am I really in prison?

How could I have just been free a few hours ago and now my life has completely changed?

What am I going to do? I have to tell my mom her daughter is behind bars.

Am I really wearing a jumpsuit like you see on TV?

My thoughts ran wild until I finally got to a place of peace. *Thank you, God, that I am finally free of the mental prison I have been in for the majority of my adult life.*

For so long, I'd felt like I wasn't good enough. I walked on eggshells, watching what I said, because I didn't want to set Kent off. I was careful how I spoke to men so he wouldn't think I was cheating on him. I had an endless list of duties I had to fulfill to maintain our relationship and keep peace between us.

Needless to say, I was scared and embarrassed to face my family because I had no idea how they would react. On Saturday, it took me a while to get up the nerve to call my parents. I was so ashamed that all I could do was cry. When I finally got up the nerve to call my mom and dad, they told me, over the sound of my crying, not to worry. They would be there for me in court on Monday. My parents didn't ask any questions. They just showed their unwavering support.

I was relieved to hear my mom say that, but I was still nervous about seeing my parents and facing the music. On Sunday, I attended the facility's Bible study and was happy to discover the ladies leading it were from my church. I sat in the back and listened to the Word, but of course, I dared not introduce myself. I had a peaceful night's sleep and anxiously awaited my court appearance. The promise of freedom rang in my ear, and I was ready for it.

● ● ●

After a long weekend, Monday finally arrived. I walked in the courtroom wearing an orange jumpsuit, shackles on my legs, and handcuffs on my wrists. Over the weekend, I hadn't once bathed because I was scared to go into the showers. I had seen one too many "soap on a rope" movie and TV scenes. Unable to look my parents in their eyes, I hung my head as I entered the courtroom. They must have been so disappointed by the way my life had turned out. After investing countless hours in my growth and development and doing everything they knew how to do to keep me on the right path, I imagined they must've wondered how their daughter could turn out like this.

I appeared before the judge, and he read the details of my case. The U.S. Attorney spoke, and then my attorney pleaded my case. This was my first offense, I had ties to the community, and I wasn't a flight risk, he explained. He made every argument he could make on my behalf. This was my first time meeting him, but I was profoundly grateful for how he showed up for me. He was articulate and professional, and he knew the law.

My attorney made his arguments convincingly, and the judge released me on bond with several stipulations. I would be under house arrest and subject to pretrial monitoring. And I was to have no contact at all—not face to face, email, text messaging, phone calls, telegrams, or smoke signals—with Kent. I would have agreed to whatever terms the judge set. I just wanted to be free.

My parents and I rode home with tension and confusion hanging between us. They were trying to figure out how to ask me in a nice way what the hell I was doing, and I was trying to figure out some way to explain how I got myself into this situation. I didn't know where to start or what to say, but I'd have to figure it out.

Every story has an end, but in life every ending is a new beginning.

DAKOTA FANNING IN *UPTOWN GIRLS*

Chapter 9
A New Beginning

The day I was released on bond, I moved back into my parents' house with just the clothes I had on my back. My room looked the same as it had when I left, except it was much cleaner and had a new bed and a few different furniture pieces. My future was unsure—not the blank slate that lay before me when I graduated college and could choose any direction I wanted for my life, but one big question mark. It was not only largely out of my control but also out of my parents' control. I was anxious about the upcoming court dates and what my fate would be.

My parents and I immediately sat down and reviewed the terms of my pretrial release. I had to maintain a job or be a full-time student. I had curfew guidelines and had to check in weekly with the probation officer. I was subject to random drug tests and basically had to do everything the court asked of me. I enrolled in a project management class for construction, started working in the family construction business, got counseling, and threw myself into work and school.

We didn't discuss what I would say to people about why I had moved back home. However, I knew not to tell anyone about the case. Instead, I told people I'd broken up with my boyfriend and needed some time to focus on rebuilding my life, which was, of course, also true.

Not surprisingly, my parents expected me to adhere to every rule and obligation outlined by the court. They also expected me to participate in all the legal hearings, get As in all of my certification courses, help organize and structure the family business, and do anything else I needed to do to get my life back on track. In their minds, it was time for me to put in the work. Through this process, our parent-child relationship became much stronger. They never said, "I told you so." They never condemned me for my choices. Instead, my parents were very loving and supportive throughout my ordeal. They attended every court case, paid all my legal bills, and reminded me my life was not over because of this situation.

As for my mini mansion, with its massive closet bursting at the seams with designer everything and its three-car garage that housed two Mercedes-Benz vehicles and a Hummer, it was gone. A week after I was released from jail, the judge ordered me not to go back to the house and to leave all my prized possessions there. Practically everything I owned was seized by the government and later sold at an auction. All my material possessions were gone, and the world I once knew was gone with them. It was such a humbling experience, and it showed me the most valuable things I had in life were my faith in God and my family.

Living at home gave me a lot of time to reflect on my own life and my beliefs. One belief that shifted for me was how I viewed money. A lot of people think money will solve all their problems. Our society holds up a financially rich life as the primary goal and the way to ensure happiness, but I'm here to tell you this is not the case. For most of the time I was with Kent, I had great material possessions. I was also broken on the inside, tolerating emotional abuse, stressed about business, not eating, walking in constant fear, and always looking over my shoulder.

Kent, I realized, had never loved me. He'd simply seen me as a means to get what he wanted and to position himself where he wanted to be. With my head for business, I helped him get the status and acceptance he so desperately craved. Money, not love, had been the foundation of our relationship for him. I'd never gotten caught up in the attachment to material possessions that ruled his life, but my self-esteem had been so low that I'd lived by his standard for all those years. Money was indeed a tool, and he'd used it, along with lies and emotional manipulation, to control me.

My life with Kent was not a life of total prosperity. Total prosperity is when you are whole and peaceful and have joy in your mind, body, and spirit. Money is not the root of evil, as so many people misquote 1 Timothy 6:10. Money didn't rob me of my self-respect, my dignity, or my self-worth. *The love of money* is the root of all evil. Money is neither good nor bad until you put it into a person's hands. Money amplifies who you are. If you are a giver, the more money you have, the more money you will give. If you are stingy and selfish, the more you have, the more you will hoard.

Money doesn't change the essence or character of who you are. It reveals and magnifies it. Acquiring more money didn't make my relationship with my ex-boyfriend better, and it didn't keep me out of legal trouble.

In addition to adjusting to life back in my parents' home, at thirty years old, I had Big Brother looking over my shoulder. My probation officer monitored my every move through an electronic bracelet. I didn't recognize how much I valued my freedom to come and go as I pleased until I no longer had it. Being monitored added another layer of stress on my circumstances. If traffic slowed to a near stop, making me late coming home from school, I had to notify my probation officer. If I needed to leave the house before my designated release time, I had to notify the officer. My life was totally monitored, and every step I made was controlled. Just as bad, this electronic bracelet on my ankle was not a cute fashion accessory. I couldn't wear dresses, skirts, or shorts—unless I wanted to draw attention and unwanted questions—and the leg of my jeans often rolled up because it couldn't lie flat over the bracelet.

Shortly after the arrest, my attorney and my mother both suggested I attend counseling to sort through how I'd ended up here and to process the present problems and the uncertainty of my future. It didn't take much convincing to get me on board with the idea. I did my research, looking for a counselor who could meet me where I was. I needed someone wise and experienced but also firm, who wouldn't allow me to wallow in self-pity. After speaking to more than a dozen counselors, I finally settled on the right one.

Our first session changed my life. The counselor said, "I'll give you this one session, and this one session only, to talk about your ex-boyfriend and what he did. The rest of our sessions will be focused on why you didn't have boundaries and allowed yourself to be treated this way." If I was looking for firm, I'd found it, and this new perspective shaped how I handled my situation from that day forward. I could no longer lay my problems at Kent's feet. I had to own my part. I had to accept that I was an adult with free will. I'd chosen to say yes when I could have, and should have, said no. I'd chosen to give him an unreasonable amount of power over me. Now I had to do the work, figure out why, and begin to heal and become the woman I wanted to be.

Of course, my family didn't see it that way because they loved me and knew I'd been raised to know the difference between right and wrong. They blamed Kent because they'd known from the beginning that he wasn't good for me. Early on, they'd looked right through him and seen the manipulation behind what I thought was generosity, the possessiveness behind what I thought was charm. Wiser and more experienced, they'd tried to warn me, but couldn't do much to steer me away from him. She'd never admit it, but I'm sure my mother prayed every type of "Get him, Jesus!" prayer she could think of because I was her baby girl and she wanted more for me.

Counseling helped me examine my role in creating my situation and gave me the tools to understand my behavior patterns. I had to recognize how passive I'd become in my relationship with Kent and how I'd quickly come to feel like I didn't have a voice with him, just as I'd felt unheard as a child. Although my parents did give me choices, I'd always felt like I needed to choose what they wanted for me. Where someone else might have reacted to feeling controlled with real rebellion, I became a people pleaser at an early age.

That desire to avoid conflict and confrontation by giving the people I love what they want carried over into my first serious romantic relationship, and it cost me dearly. Every time I overlooked Kent's lies or the inconsistencies in our relationship, I gave him permission to continue his bad behavior. Every time I allowed him to disrespect me, I disrespected myself. My self-worth as a woman and a person diminished day by day, year by year.

My self-esteem wasn't based on who I was or my inherent value as a child of God, but on who the man in my life said I was. I allowed him to call me out of my name and dishonor me with his words and his actions in ways that cut at the very core of who I was. Every time he tore me down, I processed this information in the fiber of my being. As a result, I started to believe I wasn't smart enough or talented enough. I believed I was immature and unable to stand on my own. I believed I wasn't pretty enough or woman enough. All because he said so. All because I didn't know who I was or what I wanted in my life. Since my self-concept was weak, I allowed him to define it for me. Since my self-worth was low, I looked to him to make me feel better about myself. I wanted acceptance, approval, love, and validation from him because I couldn't give them to myself.

I had allowed my positive belief that anything was possible for me to shift to a belief that this was the hand I was dealt in life. I had resigned myself to living in an unfulfilling relationship and running a business because someone else wanted me to run it. I'd accepted a life way beneath what I once knew I deserved and could create for myself.

At my core, I always knew I was worthy of more. I wanted to step out of fear, leave the relationship behind, and go get the life I desired. At the same time, I had invested so much in Kent, and I wanted to see that investment pay off. That dissonance kept me stuck, scared, overwhelmed, and confused.

When I tell you counseling helped me finally confront my feelings and beliefs and shift from a place of anger, regret, and shame to a place of compassion and forgiveness, that's an understatement. Counseling also helped me look at my ex-boyfriend's behavioral patterns and see a history of low self-esteem and inferiority on his part—realities he would never have admitted but which I couldn't deny. During our relationship, Kent often said his dad favored his brother over him, and I believe that belief had a huge impact on his life. He always felt he had to prove something, and he'd go to extreme lengths to do it.

71

My counselor helped me see that because he didn't have control over his own life and hadn't addressed his negative and toxic beliefs, Kent felt the need to control me. It was easier for him to project his own issues onto me than it would have been for him to deal with them internally. I had asked him on several occasions to go to counseling, and his answer was always no. Kent insisted the counselor would side with me, and it would be a waste of time, and he was partly right. It would have been time wasted, not because any counselor would be biased, but because he was unwilling to take any accountability for his behavior and had no desire for self-reflection or personal transformation.

Even though I was going through this life-altering legal situation and couldn't be sure how it would turn out, I was able to find the good in it, be empathetic, and really work on building up my self-worth. I surrounded myself with people who had my best interest at heart and consistently poured life into me. Every time the church doors opened, I was front and center.

This was a lengthy process and required high levels of commitment and effort. I had to completely retrain my thoughts by changing what I listened to, watched on television, and put in my body. I purchased tons of self-help books, including books on being assertive and asking for what you want, shifting your mindset, changing your thoughts about money, attracting the type of mate you desire, having a healthy marriage, and whatever could help me get my life back on track. I went to work.

I posted affirming notes on my mirror, in the car, in my purse, on the refrigerator, and everywhere my eyes would look. I only listened to and watched motivational content. I said positive affirmations at least three times a day. The first time I looked at myself in the mirror and talked about how smart, intelligent, giving, and worthy I was, it felt like a lie because I was still dealing with my self-defeating thoughts. However, I continued to say those affirmations every day, three or four times a day. Not only did I say them in the mirror, but I also recorded them and played them at night while I slept and listened to them throughout the day. Then something magical happened. One day, I woke up and actually believed all those positive thoughts about me and my life. The days, weeks, and months of saying them and hearing them had slowly shifted what I believed.

It's often said that it takes at least twenty-one days to change a habit. Some research says sixty or ninety days, so let's just go with a month. I've found this time frame to be essential to living the life you deserve. It takes at least one month of doing something new, every single day without missing a day, to shift your mindset or change a habit. If you miss a day, you have to start all over.

This process didn't end for me when thirty days were up. I worked on changing my mindset, day in and day out, for years. I'd carried so many toxic thoughts and beliefs since childhood, and not only were they not serving me, but they weren't even true. Whenever negative thoughts came into my mind, I replaced them with positive thoughts. Whenever something negative came out of my mouth, I contradicted it with something positive. Whenever I did something wrong or something didn't help me become who I wanted to be, I admitted it, took ownership of it, apologized if necessary, and did something different.

Becoming a new me took dedication, effort, and a complete investment in changing my beliefs and thoughts, which would change my actions. So many people stay stuck right where they are because it's easier to just exist than to take a risk and have the chance to thrive. I couldn't afford to do that any longer. I'd finally made a decision to become someone different.

I had to take a hard look at myself and be honest about not liking the person I saw in the mirror. I had a "come to Jesus" moment with myself and performed a reality check. In my heart of hearts, I was a confident and bold woman who pursued the life she wanted and got it, but I couldn't see her clearly yet. In my day-to-day reality, I was an insecure, emotionally fragile, broken, and scared little girl trapped inside of a woman's body—but I was growing and changing.

Initially, I had to step out in faith because other people believed in me more than I believed in myself. I didn't see the person they saw. Fortunately, they spoke life into me to help me develop my self-belief. One of my closest girlfriends ran down a list of my accomplishments. She asked me, "Who worked to build the business? Who took the marketing and business courses? Who created the strategic partnerships?

Who put blood, sweat, and tears into the business and the relationship? Do you not believe God would reward you for that?" She let those questions sink in, and then she continued. "Look at who you have become because of this. There's greatness inside of you, just bursting at the seams. All you have to do is let it out."

Her words spoke to me and stirred my spirit. Her act of compassion showed me the power of someone else speaking greatness over your life when you don't believe it yourself. It may be a friend, a coach, or a family member. Those words may even come from a stranger on the street or in line at the grocery store or even from someone you've never meet in person.

Around this time, I was listening to Joyce Meyer, a Bible teacher and author focused on helping people enjoy living a better life, and she said something so powerful, which spoke directly to me. She said, "You will always reap *what* you sow, but not necessarily *where* you sow." It took me a minute to process what she said, but once I got it, I got it.

All the years and effort I'd sown into the businesses and the relationship weren't wasted. No, I didn't receive the harvest I wanted from my ex-boyfriend or those businesses, but I would receive the harvest in my future husband and future businesses. Hallelujah, and thank you, Lawd! This realization put a fire up under my behind, and I was ready to take on the world.

I couldn't live my life stuck in the past, complaining about what should have happened, who should have loved me, what should have worked out. The past was the past, and it would never change. I had to accept it, forgive myself and others, grieve the life I'd lost, and expect to receive a harvest for all the good seeds I'd sown. It took me some time, but eventually I started to see the greatness in me and applied myself to making sure that greatness materialized in my life. The next year would be grueling, with court dates, depositions, and de-briefings, but there would also be a wonderful turn of events.

True love does not come by finding the perfect person but by learning to see an imperfect person perfectly.

JASON JORDAN

Chapter 10
The Queen Meets Her King

M y thirties sure didn't start the way I'd expected. My closest confidant was my attorney; the people I talked to most were my probation officer and representatives from the United States Attorney's office. There had to be a silver lining somewhere in this story, and I was determined to find it.

To get my mind off the case, I immersed myself in reading, studying, and listening to all types of self-help and motivational material. I had a keen interest in marriage and family, and I wanted to set myself up for a future in which I would have both. As I was learning about how to attract my ideal mate and have a healthy marriage, I decided to write out a list of what I wanted in a husband. When I finished, I had a twelve-page, typed list of what I desired in my future husband. I was very detailed about everything from his spirituality and character to his ambition and parenting skills, what he ate, and how he treated me. I wanted to be specific and intentional about my next relationship because I hadn't been in the past.

I'd accepted what was given to me and lost myself in the process. This time, I wanted to have clear boundaries and clear goals for my relationship.

Because I'd learned to identify and own my part in my relationship with , I also invested a lot of time in getting clear about what I would bring to my future relationship. Once I knew what I wanted, I spent a lot of time researching what made marriages work or fail. I wanted to go in with my eyes wide open about the work required to build a happy marriage. I did all this with no specific man in mind and no potential suitors. But when the right man came along, I would be ready.

While I prayed one day, God asked me if I could offer a man all those things on my list of what I wanted from my future husband, and I had to be honest. My answer was no. So God asked me how I could expect to attract a man who had more to offer than I did. That was a good point. I started to work harder than ever on changing and growing to become the type of mate I wanted to attract.

I put my list down and asked God to lead me and make me the wife He wanted me to be, and I prayed my future husband would be led and shaped by God too. Daily, my prayer was: "God, make me into the wife You have called me to be, and make my future husband into the husband You have called him to be. Prepare us, and when we are both ready, let us meet. Let me recognize him in the Spirit, and let him recognize me in the Spirit. Let him pursue me because a man who findeth a wife findeth a good thing." I also opened myself up to the idea that my husband might not come in the package I expected him to. Even though my list was twelve pages, I gave God leeway to send me who He felt I needed.

One Sunday, I sat in church listening to the pastor teach about the roles of a husband and a wife. After the service was over, I looked to my right and saw a very handsome man, clean-shaven with a sexy bald head, caramel skin, and a beautiful smile. He was dressed in a nice pair of slacks with a striped button-down shirt and nicely polished shoes. I checked him out from head to toe and really liked what I saw. He introduced himself as Anthony, and he and I struck up a conversation as we left the sanctuary.

As we walked out, an old friend called out to me. My friend and I chatted for a bit, but as we talked, I continued to walk towards Anthony so he and I wouldn't lose contact (whenever Anthony tells the story he says I chased after him). As soon as my friend departed, Anthony and I picked up our conversation. We talked about where we were from, how long we'd each attended the church, and what we did for a living. After about thirty minutes, he offered me his card. I told him thanks but no thanks. If we were going to talk further, he would need to call me. I wrote my number on the back of the card and returned it to him. We talked for a few more minutes and went separate ways to our cars.

I'd done so much to rebuild my confidence, so I expected him to call me that night, but he waited a few days before he called. When we finally got on the phone, we talked for over three hours. He and I were both in a place of starting anew. We were both rebuilding, and neither of us was looking for a relationship. Each of us just wanted a friend to talk to while we focused on our own lives.

I really enjoyed our first conversation because Anthony was very easy to talk to, intellectual, and asked great questions. We discussed so many different things. He told me he was divorced and raising his daughter. We went through what had happened in his life and how his daughter ended up staying with him, and his decision and ability to stand up and take responsibility for his daughter impressed me. I was really intrigued with him at this point.

A couple of nights went by, and no call from Anthony. I didn't think much of it, at first, but this pattern repeated several times. We would talk for hours, and then he wouldn't call for two or three days. I wasn't sure what was happening, but I didn't like it. It seemed like his interest in our friendship wasn't strong or consistent, so I took a page from my brother's book and deleted Anthony's number.

When Anthony called several days later, I asked, "Who is this?" He answered with his name, and I replied, "Oh, I'm sorry. I deleted your number." This must have gotten his attention—perhaps he thought I was the one losing interest—because he finally asked me out.

After talking on the phone for weeks, we went out on our first date. We met at a Barnes & Noble bookstore, but neither of us could remember exactly what the other one looked like. We each waited in different parts of the store so we could see the other walking in the door. Anthony arrived before I did, so he was already in the back of the bookstore. I came through the side Starbucks door and went straight to the business section.

Finally, Anthony called me on the phone to see where I was, and I asked him to meet me at the front of the bookstore. I waited until he got there so I could see what he looked like. "Just as I remember," I said, "as handsome as ever," and he said, "You're as cute as I remember." We both were pleased with what we saw, and off we went to Red Lobster.

At dinner, we enjoyed great conversation as I stuffed my face with the cheddar biscuits, I love (well, used to love since I'm eating a gluten-free diet these days). It should have been just like any other great first date, but one distraction kept pulling my attention away. My jeans kept rising because of that darn ankle bracelet.

I hadn't said anything at all to Anthony about my legal woes, so I didn't want him to see my little secret. He had no idea I was on probation, and since he and I were both just looking for a friend, I saw no reason to bring it up. Not much was going on with my case; I was waiting to hear about the next steps, so I didn't want to get involved in a long discussion about it. I just wanted to be in the moment, so I did my best to ignore the monitor and focus on the handsome man across the table from me.

Anthony and I continued to talk and hang out. We went to Bible study and church together, and we built a great friendship. Our relationship started off slow and casual, but it wouldn't stay that way.

Relationships are always stronger when you are best friends first and a couple second.

AUTHOR UNKNOWN

Chapter 11
The Speed of Lightning

I don't know how we moved out of the friend zone, but we did. Our relationship progressed quickly, and I developed serious feelings for Anthony. It's funny because the package God sent him in was very different from what I'd envisioned. If I hadn't been in prayer and open to God's will, I would have missed Anthony completely.

I asked God for a man who had never been married and had no kids, and He gave me divorced with a teenage daughter. I asked God for established and financially secure, and He gave me rebuilding and reestablishing credit. I asked for six-foot-three with a head full of hair, and He gave me six feet and bald. I asked God for an aggressive entrepreneur, and He gave me a hard-working, smart, progressive, and loyal person, who couldn't care less about owning his own business and preferred a stable, advancing, and rewarding career. Now, don't get me wrong. Anthony would build a business on the side, but he preferred to also have a steady income instead of relying solely on the unpredictable revenues that typically come in the first five years of building a business.

God has a huge sense of humor, and He laughed at me when I gave Him my wish list. He knew who He had for me without my list, and in the end, I was glad God sent me what He knew I needed instead of what I thought I wanted. Sometimes it's much easier to let go, completely trust God, and let Him drive than it is to depend on our own intellectual expertise. That was the case for me as I baby-stepped my way towards a new relationship.

Deep down, I knew I had to tell Anthony about my legal troubles, but it wasn't the type of information that came up naturally in conversation. We had only been dating for a couple of months, but each of us had found something special in the other. We could talk about anything and really had fun together. We prayed together and studied the Word. Plus, we had amazing chemistry—physically, mentally, emotionally, and spiritually. In a nutshell, he was the full package, and I believed this was the man I was supposed to marry.

Yes, I had said I only wanted to be friends, but my mind changed quickly. I wanted to seal the deal, and seal it fast, with this handsome, smart, hardworking man, but of course, I was going to let him lead and make the first move. In the meantime, I had to figure out how to let him in on the details of my legal situation even though I still had no final resolution.

The dreaded day came one Saturday when we were hanging out at Anthony's apartment. I sat him down and told him I needed to discuss something serious with him. There was a chance that it would end our budding relationship, but he deserved to know the challenges I was facing before our involvement became any more serious.

In his efforts to lighten the mood, Anthony asked, "You aren't a man, are you?" I assured him I wasn't. Then he asked, "Did you kill your ex-boyfriend?" Once again, I said no. Anthony said, "Okay. If it's not either of those two things, you can tell me anything."

We laughed and joked, and then I confessed. Well, I actually didn't confess everything, just a little bit. I didn't tell him all the nitty-gritty details. I just brushed the surface and said I was in some legal trouble with one of the businesses I had owned with a partner. We were going through a legal case, I explained, but at worst, I could expect to get some time on probation.

Those words had no right to come out of my mouth because my attorney had never told me that. Instead, he'd assured me he and his team would work the case with all their resources and strive to create the best outcome, which could, in fact, include some prison time for me. Even though my attorney had been quite clear, my mind had latched on to the word probation. It was the best I could hope for, and it was what I expected, so that's exactly what I told Anthony.

"We're still going through all the legal preliminaries," I explained, "but I hope it'll all be over soon so I can put it behind me."

Anthony was very understanding. He actually said it made him like me even more because it showed I had some grit and wasn't as prim and proper as he'd thought. To my relief, he was very supportive about the whole thing.

● ● ●

Just as our relationship was heating up, so was my case. My former boyfriend had been arrested and brought into custody. Apparently, he'd attempted to flee the country and had a knock-down-drag-out with the police, all of which I found out when a girlfriend called to tell me Kent had made the nightly news for assaulting an officer and resisting arrest. A judge initially denied Kent bail, but after he appealed, he was released on house arrest. At this point, I was so far removed from him, that the news seemed more like a reality TV show than anything to do with my life.

In the upcoming weeks, there were several court hearings scheduled, and one court appearance totally blew my mind. It changed my perspective on how I saw our ten-year relationship when through the courtroom door walked a younger version of me, hair in the same style, same True Religion jeans and T-shirt Kent had bought for me, same Chuck Taylor Converse shoes, same Gucci purse, same everything from head to toe. The only difference was the stroller she was pushing and the baby girl in it. From one look at this young woman, I could tell she had no idea what she'd gotten herself into.

Before that moment, I'd had a very different idea of what my ex-boyfriend's wife would look like because of what he'd told me about her. In one of the very weird and inappropriate conversations I had with him after we broke up, Kent asked me if I wanted to know how he and his new wife met. I said no, but he proceeded to tell me anyway.

For some reason, even though we weren't together anymore, he was trying to make me jealous, and he told me they met online. I assumed Kent meant a dating website, like Match or eHarmony, but he explained it was a prostitution site. Kent was known for stretching the truth at times, so I couldn't be sure if this was accurate information or not. I just took his word for it. He went on to explain their relationship started off sexual, but then he would pay her to go to the movies or hang out with him, and it blossomed into more. This made absolutely no sense to me, and the conversation got weirder by the minute.

I'm not one to judge, but so many thoughts ran through my head. I wondered what in the world was going on in his mind that he felt he needed to pay someone to go to the movies with him. Kent had a way of charming the pants off you and selling you very big dreams, and he wasn't hard on the eyes. Finding a date was never a challenge for him. So armed with this knowledge of him and the information he shared about his wife, I expected something totally different. I always assumed she saw the big cars, houses, and money and wanted the lifestyle. Kent believed in spending lots of money and showering his woman with gifts, trips, fine restaurants, and extravagant jewelry, and I assumed that all appealed to her. Of course, she got much more than she bargained for with a huge legal case looming over her life, and she was caught in the middle because the attorneys believed she was helping him hide assets, which brings us back to the day I laid eyes on her.

They were both supposed to appear in court that day, but Kent's wife showed up without him. In her, I saw a scared little girl trapped in a woman's body, just as I had been when I was with him. As I sat there looking at her, I realized my ex-boyfriend was once again searching for a younger woman he could mold and manipulate. It wasn't about finding a partner to grow with him. It was about control. When she explained how he had dropped her off to come into court for the two of them, instead of being a man and her protector and facing the music, it reminded me of how he had thrown me to the wolves many times to defend myself when his actions had gotten us in the situation.

When she talked about how he wooed her and shared the details of their relationship, it was like a replay of what had happened with us. The only difference: he spent more lavishly with her because, in the beginning of our relationship, we only had a few pennies to rub together. From her hairstyle to how she dressed to the way she talked she was a carbon copy of me. Early on, Kent had told me I talked too country and worked with me on changing my speech. I assumed he'd done the same with her.

Kent had also told me my first name was too ethnic to use in business. He and I had only been dating for a year or so when we started our first business. When we went to networking events or gave presentations, my first name, Tameka, rubbed him the wrong way. Several studies reported an ethnic name on a resume often prevented a candidate from getting a job interview, so it seemed like he might be right about my name.

Kent would often say, "If we want to do big business, we need a big business image to match." One day, he designed new business cards for us, and mine had the name T. Reneé on them. Tameka had been reduced to a T with no input from me. He suggested (well, more like ordered) that I start going by the new name. I didn't think too much of it at the time because I was reading articles about names influencing advancement, so I went along with it. My parents, friends, and family, of course, still called me by my first name; I only used the new name in business. In retrospect, I'm amazed by how many little and big things he changed about me and how I went along with it all.

My heart opened with compassion for his wife. She was left to raise two kids, their daughter and a son from a previous relationship, by herself. She had stepped into what appeared to be a wonderful, lavish life, and she ended up getting a nightmare. I didn't speak with her, but I prayed for her from afar.

Then things got really interesting. Just a short time after attending the court hearings, while on house arrest, my ex-boyfriend cut off his ankle monitor and fled the country. He was running from the law, so this couldn't end well. Months went by, but he was eventually captured and extradited back to Atlanta. But his return wasn't the end of my troubles.

From this day forward you shall not walk alone. May my heart be your shelter and my arms be your home.

MARIANNE WILLIAMSON

Chapter 12
Wedding Bells

M y courtship with Anthony moved fast. After we realized we wanted to build a life together, I wanted my parents to meet him. Because of my previous relationship, they'd booted me off the "find a husband" committee. My mother was chairperson, and my father was co-chairperson. Their opinions mattered more than ever.

Anthony's first encounter with my mom turned out to be a bit tense. My mom and I were shopping at a mall near Anthony's house, so he dropped by for a casual meeting. Within a few breaths, my mom asked, "What are your intentions with my daughter?" She said I wasn't young, and if he wasn't interested in marriage, he shouldn't waste my time.

Hello. I'm standing right here, Mom. Can you be a little more discreet? I was only thirty-one, and my mom was acting like I was going on seventy.

Anthony laughed and gave some politically correct answer, but my mother continued to be very direct and said what was on her mind. When we were alone, I asked my mom her initial thoughts of Anthony, and she said, "He seemed nice. We'll see."

The second meeting between Anthony and my mom was a lot more relaxed. He came over to my parents' house for dinner, and they had a chance to talk to him and learn more about him. In a very short period of time, my family got to know Anthony well. Fortunately, they liked him.

As he got to know my family and we grew closer, Anthony and I talked more about building a life together. We discussed our values, our desire for more children, our career and business paths, finances, and spirituality. Within about three months of dating, we started to look at engagement rings. While it was fast by many standards, I was all in, and Anthony was too. We each thought we had found our soulmate.

As my mother's birthday approached, Anthony suggested we plan a nice dinner for the family. I wanted to do something a little different, so we made reservations at a Moroccan restaurant with authentic cuisine, fire dancers, and all the traditional trimmings.

Back at my parents' house after dinner, Anthony and I were talking in the den when he got down on one knee and proposed to me. He presented me with a princess cut diamond engagement ring with little diamond baguettes on each side of the center stone, proving his listening skills because this was the exact ring I'd described to him. It was the ring I'd always dreamed of having when I got engaged.

We'd only been dating four months, and while we'd discussed the possibility of marriage, the proposal caught me off guard. I later found out Anthony had already spoken with my parents about his desire to propose to me. He was very traditional and had sat down with them and asked for my hand in marriage, and they had given him their blessing.

Through tears of joy and happiness, I said the only thing I could say. I said yes because I loved this man and wanted to spend the rest of my life with him. I had known both things within three weeks of meeting him. God had showed me His favor by providing me with such a man so well suited for me and what I wanted and needed in a relationship. I was smiling from ear to ear as I ran screaming through the house, showing off my ring and posing while my mom took pictures. My parents seemed delighted.

● ◌ ●

After the engagement was official, my mom wanted to start planning a wedding. Everyone was excited about my upcoming nuptials, but no one more than her. She had waited her whole life to plan her dream wedding for me. She was going to live vicariously through me, and she was going to enjoy it.

My father had a different way of looking at things. While my mother laid out her ideas for what would make my wedding special, he asked me if I wanted a wedding or a down payment on a house. Of course, being raised by two people who taught me the value of a dollar, and having lost the home I'd purchased, I said I'd prefer a down payment on a house. When she heard my answer, my mother looked cross-eyed at me.

Then my dad asked what about a small down payment on a house and a small wedding, and I said, "Great!" Again, my mother gave me a stare that made it clear I'd given the wrong answer. We would be planning a wedding, and we'd be doing it her way. The date we chose gave us seven months to plan the ceremony and reception. In essence, within one year of meeting, Anthony and I would be husband and wife.

Planning a wedding turned out to be a lot harder than I'd expected, so we solicited the help of a wedding directress and a creative director. Throughout this process, I saw skills in my mother that I hadn't realized she possessed. She had impeccable taste and original ideas, and her choices were effortlessly exquisite. She would have made an exceptional wedding planner had she ever decided to pursue that career.

I had so much fun, from food tasting to anticipating my bachelorette party that I got lost in the moment. I put aside thoughts and worries about my legal case and focused on my fairy-tale wedding and my future marriage. It amazed me that I had existed in such a toxic relationship for ten years and then God blessed me with the most amazing husband in the world. It was clear to me that dreams do come true, and I was able to enjoy every minute of this dream because my mother took on so much of the planning work.

From the dress to the ceremony to the reception, my mother made me feel like a princess. In our search for my wedding dress, we spent one Friday morning visiting several bridal shops. I saw some gorgeous dresses, but I didn't fall in love with any of them. We were just about to call it a day when we went into the final bridal store on our list, and there it was.

The dress consultant brought us three different dresses to look at, and one immediately drew my attention. The bright white strapless gown with a heart-shaped neckline, a fitted waist, and a corset that laced up the back had a long, graceful train and looked like it had come straight out of *Vogue* magazine. I was in love, and when I tried on the gown with a sparkling tiara and elegant veil, I looked and felt like a queen.

Once we had my gown, I wanted to make sure the groom, bridesmaids, and groomsmen were on point. My husband didn't ask for much input in our wedding, but he did ask to choose the attire for his groomsmen and himself, and he handled that. I always hated buying a bridesmaid's dress I could never wear again, so I made sure my girls wouldn't have that problem. With my pink-and-silver color scheme in mind, my mom and I found a pink strapless fitted dress with a flared skirt. My maid of honor's dress was a little different from the bridesmaids' dresses, but they all fell in love with the dresses, especially since they were suitable for other events. Of course, my AKA (Alpha Kappa Alpha) bridesmaids agreed with the color selection. I'm a Delta (Delta Sigma Theta), but we look good in pink too.

At one of my favorite hotels near the airport, my mother and I toured a venue for the reception. During the tour, we were treated to a food tasting, and every dish was to live for, even the salad. I tasted everything on the menu, except the beef, before we made our final selections. The menu consisted of sautéed chicken with spinach and rice or a selection of beef with a salad and green beans. We ordered a three-tiered bridal cake, topped with a couple that looked madly in love just like Anthony and I were, and a two-tiered groom's cake.

To add a special touch to our wedding, we did a full photo shoot with a celebrity photographer. I'd attended weddings where I knew the bride or the groom but had no idea how they met, so we had a photo montage created of our relationship and shot a "how we met" video, in which we talked about meeting, what we each thought was special about the other, and what we looked forward to as a couple. This video would play during the reception so each side of our family could get to know us as a couple on a more personal level.

The invitations and wedding programs were elegant and luxurious. My mother pulled out the etiquette books and made sure every invitation had tissue paper in it and an addressed and stamped return envelope for the RSVP. Now if it had been up to me, I would have let guests text or email their RSVP, but my mom wasn't having any of that. This wedding would be first class all the way.

As we ramped up to the big day, my mother focused on the wedding while Anthony and I worked on building a life together. We attended premarital counseling and found out some interesting things about each other that hadn't come up in all our deep conversations. The counseling also gave us a good understanding of marriage and how to create a solid foundation for our relationship. We went to counseling for about eight weeks, but knowing what I know today, we should have gone for at least *eighty* weeks. Every couple should. But we were young and in love, and if nothing else, I was doing things in a much healthier way than I'd done in my previous relationship.

Finally, it was pre-wedding party time, so Anthony and his best man, his brother, went into planning mode for Anthony's bachelor party. Not to be outdone, my girls set the stage for the best bachelorette party ever. The details about these parties are still under lock and key and as confidential as a matter of national security. Let me just say Anthony and I both had a good time at our last hurrahs before we jumped the broom. My girls sure know how to throw a party.

● ◦ ●

The wedding day finally arrived, and our ceremony took place at the church I grew up in. When I walked into the sanctuary before getting dressed, what I saw was enchanting. At the front of the church stood an altar with four large columns draped with beautiful white fabric and flowers. Lush flower arrangements in pink and silver with accents of ivory decorated the pews and the rest of the space, and candles flickered throughout the sanctuary. Taking it all in, I admired the breathtaking loveliness and once again counted my blessings.

On my way down to the dressing room, I felt both the adrenaline of excitement and butterflies in my stomach as I anxiously waited to become Mrs. Smith. As the time drew near, my mom guided me up the stairs to make my grand entrance. The music started to play, and a tear welled in my dad's eye. I asked him if everything was okay, and he said, "Yes, it's fine. I must have something in my eye." That was such a sweet moment for me because my dad was so proud of his little girl and so pleased with my choice of a husband.

As my father and I started our walk down the aisle, I focused on the big smile on Anthony's face. I couldn't wait to stand by his side. The soloist sang, "God Made You Just for Me" in a way that touched hearts, including mine. I had broken down crying in rehearsal the night before, but I made it through the ceremony. Finally, the preacher said, "I now pronounce you husband and wife," and Anthony and I kissed and walked down the aisle as newlyweds, waving and smiling to all the special people in our lives who had come to share this day with us.

The guests left the church and headed to the hotel for the reception, and Anthony and I made our way right behind them in a vintage Rolls Royce, a wonderful wedding gift from my brother. (Let me be clear. He *rented* the Rolls Royce for the wedding; he didn't buy us a Rolls Royce.)

Anthony and I arrived at the hotel, where beautiful pictures of us decorated the space outside the ballroom. The creative director had done an amazing job with the reception decorations, from the chairs and centerpieces to the cake and gift tables. He'd made every dollar stretch a long way, and it looked like the reception for a celebrity or basketball star. Everything was upscale and flawless.

We danced, laughed, cried, and had a magical night with friends and family. It was everything I ever could have dreamed of for my wedding day. It was a day we will forever remember. Of course, our wedding night was amazing, and then we were off to the islands for a relaxing honeymoon, followed by the excitement and the agony of our new life together.

You are free to choose, but you are not free from the consequence of your choice.

EZRA TAFT BENSON

Chapter 13
Judgment Day

Just a few months after our wedding, I found out I was pregnant. Anthony and I were both overjoyed, and our families were elated. However, this joy was short-lived.

Throughout the previous year, while on pretrial probation, I'd gone back and forth to court. From the beginning, my attorney encouraged me to take a plea because a trial could result in a conviction on more serious charges and harsher sentencing than I expected to receive if I pleaded to the lesser charges. I had no desire to gamble with my freedom, so I took the deal without hesitation and happily took a plea.

Just a few months after Anthony and I were married, my sentencing date came up. That day, I woke up early and immediately hit the floor on my knees to pray. Then, I put on a pin-striped, navy-blue suit and pulled my hair back in a ponytail. Anthony and I didn't say much to each other—except that we were both believing God that I would receive probation.

We arrived in the courtroom with my parents, my brother, a family friend, and my attorney. These were the only people in my life who really knew about the case since I'd kept it under wraps around most of my friends and extended family. Inside, we waited for the judge to speak. When she called my name, she also called my co-defendant's name.

I hadn't seen Kent in almost two years. He had lost a lot of weight and looked very pale. Seeing him, I felt nothing, no emotions at all. I looked at the back of his head with a blank stare as if I were looking right through him. We never made eye contact or spoke to one another. It felt so good to be free of any feelings about him; all his control over me was gone. What a wonderful, wonderful change and a testament to my spiritual journey, on which I was learning to trust God and surrender.

I kept my attention on the judge. I had never seen her or heard of her, but we'd later learn she had a reputation as a very tough judge who didn't give leniency. The U.S. Attorney presented his case first, and then my attorney presented my case. Because of my plea deal, there was a guideline in place for my sentencing. I could receive probation, on the low end, or up to thirty years in prison.

After both attorneys had their say, the judge spoke and told me to stand for my sentencing. I stood next to my attorney, who assured me everything was going to be all right. I couldn't help wondering if he believed those words himself. My future was in the hands of someone who knew very little about me, and a fear struck me and left me numb.

The judge asked me a few questions, and I responded. The words she spoke next shook me to the core. "You are hereby sentenced to forty-six months in federal prison. You will be given time to get your affairs in order and will report within sixty days."

My knees gave way as my mother's screams filled my ears, blotting out all other sound. "Oh no! My baby!" she cried. I couldn't bear to turn and look at my husband. I didn't want to see his face and know what he was thinking. This should have been the happiest time in our life together—newlyweds, expecting our first child, excited about building our future. Instead of basking in these joys, Anthony had to prepare for life without his new wife. And I had to prepare myself to give up my freedom and serve a prison sentence just shy of four years—and to deliver my first child behind prison walls.

● ● ●

Just a few days after the sentencing, my husband and I went for a drive and had a candid conversation about our future together. I told him, "Honey, I know this isn't what you signed up for when we got married, and I know you have needs. If you want to walk away now, I completely understand."

In response, Anthony said something so profound to me that I will never forget it. "Why would I make a permanent decision that would affect our marriage based on a temporary situation?" he asked. I should have known right then and there the type of man I'd married.

Over the next several weeks, Anthony and I did our best to hold up under the stress of the date looming over us. I couldn't wrap my head around the fact that I was about to leave my family for several years, but since this train was moving and not stopping, I had to get ready for it. Kent had received a sentence almost four times the length of mine, but I took no pleasure in his punishment, and it offered me no relief.

On top of the morning sickness I suffered, my hormones were all over the place. One minute, I was happy and secure, knowing we'd all be together again in a few years, and the next, my mind raced, trying to come to terms with what was about to happen. I couldn't think logically. I felt scared, nervous, and overwhelmed with so many concerns. *Will my marriage really survive? Will I have a healthy baby? How can I adjust to life away from my family? How will my new family make it financially?* My questions went on and on.

I tirelessly researched the federal facility where I would be spending the next few years of my life, finding out every detail available to the public. I also visited the halfway house I'd return to after serving my sentence and talked to the staff about the expectations there. I needed to get some insight into this new world my unborn child and I would inhabit.

Through it all, Anthony and I tried to stay focused and prepare ourselves as best we could for the arrival of our new baby and my departure. This, by far, was the best and worst of times in my life. The fairy-tale wedding was over, and a journey I never wanted to go on was about to begin.

*Not everyone will understand
your journey. That's fine. It's not
their journey to make sense of.
It's yours.*

ZERO DEAN

Chapter 14
The Journey Begins

That fateful day came when my husband and I had to rise early and drive to the prison camp in Florida. This was such a bittersweet moment for me. I had finally met the man meant to be my husband, I was pregnant with our first child together, and I was on my way to serve a forty-six-month sentence. The family life I loved and appreciated and wanted to protect was about to be tested and tried, and I didn't know if we would make it. I was just going through the motions and trying to hold everything together.

I wouldn't be away for a full four years because I'd only have to serve a portion of my sentence. However, I still had to face separation from my new family for about three years. I didn't have a whole lot of information about where I would give birth or what would happen once my child was born. I just prayed I'd receive appropriate prenatal care, which would allow me to have a healthy pregnancy and delivery.

On the car ride to Florida, Anthony and I kept the conversation upbeat. He reassured me that everything was going to be fine, and we talked about all the wonderful things we'd do once I was home. We agreed we would write a lot and talk every day. We both said we would use this time to strengthen our relationship with God and be strong for one another. Neither of us was visibly sad. We didn't cry. We each tried to be strong for the other.

As is the way with time, we arrived at the facility more quickly than I'd expected. With no real idea how long it would be before we embraced again, my husband and I hugged and kissed before we went in, and he held my hand as I walked to the front door to check in.

A middle-age white woman, about five-six, like me, greeted me. (I often use the term *resident* instead of inmate and *facility* instead of prison out of respect for the humanity of the residents.) Her job was to check in all new residents, and while she wasn't overly friendly, she was pleasant. She advised me the place wasn't as bad as I might think. "You'll be fine," she told me, and she gave Anthony and me a rundown of how everything worked and really helped put my mind at ease.

When the administrator called my name, she told me I could say my last goodbye to my husband, and then she would complete my paperwork and provide me with my clothing. Anthony gave me the biggest hug and kiss, he told me he loved me, and he promised me he would be with me every step of the way.

My heart dropped as my husband exited the building and drove away in his car. It was time for me to put on my big girl panties or, in this case, my khaki jumpsuit. It was time to face the music.

You never know how strong you are until being strong is your only choice.

BOB MARLEY

Chapter 15
I Don't Look So Bad in Khakis

Just a few hours earlier, I had been free to do as I pleased. I went from enjoying the sunny Florida day with my husband to suddenly confined to a nine-by-twelve cell. This came after I was checked in and experienced a full body search, during which I had to bend over and cough. (It was so invasive I hoped the baby didn't get embarrassed by the process.) Wondering how my life ended up like this, I felt violated, but prison officials had to make sure I wasn't trying to smuggle anything in. Once I was allowed to get dressed, I wore a brown khaki uniform that identified me as pregnant. The other ladies had on green khakis with army boots or tennis shoes. The sensory overload, uncertainty, and culture shock threatened to overwhelm me.

I wasn't in a hardcore prison, the kind of facility so popular as settings for Netflix shows and old late-night movies. I wouldn't be filing my toothbrush into a shank or dealing with riots. Instead, I'd been sent to a prison camp very similar to where Martha Stewart served time for insider trading. A lot of the ladies were there for white-collar crimes. Others, most of whom were serving time for drug charges, had transitioned from medium-security facilities to the camp once they were down to a few years left on their sentence.

Processing my surroundings, I noted several dormitories (my term, not the administrators') and no barbed-wire fence to prevent us from escaping. The accommodations reminded me of a very strict residence hall. The walls, the floors, and the furniture were all painted the same dull grey color. Even though it was a "camp," and not a maximum-security facility, I had no doubt that I was in prison.

My emotions bounced from fear and shock to the kind of peace only found in denial and back again. I tried to process everything and figure out how I'd cope with the facts of my circumstances. Married just seven months, four months pregnant, separated from my family, thrust into an environment where I didn't know anybody—my life had completely changed. I did my best to focus on how I'd remain sane in the midst of this chaos, reminding myself that every emotion I felt my baby would also feel. Whatever I did emotionally, physically, spiritually, or mentally would affect my unborn child.

Overall, I adjusted well. The ladies at the camp performed all the jobs—cooking, maintenance, lawn care, laundry, teaching, and whatever else needed to be done—and I got busy reading and doing my assigned jobs. It was lights on at five in the morning and out by nine at night on weekdays and eleven o'clock on the weekends. I attended Bible study, read a lot, and exercised. I found a walking buddy, and we walked three to five miles each day. The daily walks kept my mind off my circumstances and enabled me to keep fit during the pregnancy.

I tried to eat as healthy as possible, but our baby got a lot of starches. For lunch and dinner, we ate potatoes, potatoes, and potatoes. The food wasn't terrible. It was surprisingly bearable, and some days actually good, depending on which residents were cooking.

For the most part, everyone treated me nicely. Perhaps they felt sorry for me because I grew as big as a house as I gained almost sixty pounds during the pregnancy and my stomach looked like I was carrying two basketballs in it. As the weeks passed, I held up fine, and my husband was busy with work and raising our teenage daughter from his previous marriage. When we got married, she became my daughter too. She was a junior bridesmaid in our wedding, and I loved her just as if I had given birth to her. Being separated from her so soon after we became a family added to my stress.

After living at the camp for a few weeks, I had my first doctor's appointment, and the ultrasound showed I was having a boy. I knew my husband would be ecstatic because he'd always wanted a son. I called and told him the great news, and as I expected, he was overjoyed.

As my due date approached and my body prepared to give birth, I transferred from the camp to a federal facility with a program for expectant mothers. The program allowed residents to deliver in the hospital and then bond with their babies for a period of eleven months. After that time, we had to return to the camp—without our new babies—to serve the remainder of our sentences. I was excited to give birth, but nervous about what the next year had in store for me.

There has never been, nor will there ever be, anything quite so special as the love between a mother and a son.

AUTHOR UNKNOWN

Chapter 16
It's a Boy

Shortly after arriving at the program for expectant mothers, I met with the doctor, and we scheduled a day for me to be induced so my husband could attend the birth. My due date fell close to our anniversary date, so I was hoping my son would make his appearance either before or after, but not on our anniversary.

Initially, I wanted a natural birth with no epidural, but after those contractions started coming and I wasn't even dilated one centimeter, I had a change of heart. Once he was ready to make his debut, I pushed and pushed, but his head wouldn't come out, and the doctor had to use forceps. Twelve hours passed from the time I received the Pitocin and the moment of our son's arrival. I ripped a bit, but I finally delivered a healthy, eight-pound-five-ounce baby boy with my husband by my side.

Contrary to what I'd hoped, our son was born on our wedding anniversary date. This little boy came into the world knowing exactly what he wanted, and he wasn't afraid to ask for it. He arrived when he was ready, not on anyone else's timeline, and he has been a strong-willed leader since birth.

After a two-night stay, the hospital released me to go back to the mother's program, and I was absolutely devastated. The reality of life as a new mom with the sole responsibility of caring for this little person, in a place that wasn't our home and where I wouldn't have my family's support, overwhelmed me. I'd seen my husband's joy when our son was born, and I witnessed the watering of his eyes when it was time to leave.

I asked the doctor to let me stay just one more night, but even though I was still having continuous bleeding, he refused. At the time, I had no idea how skewed the health care system was against providing Black women adequate care. I didn't know Black women are less likely to be listened to by their healthcare providers or that physicians are twice as likely to discount our pain under the theory that we have a higher pain tolerance. I didn't know we're three times more likely to die from pregnancy-related causes than white women. I'm fairly certain my circumstances as a guest of the federal government didn't win me any additional respect from the doctors either. I ended up returning to the hospital for emergency surgery because my body hadn't expelled the entire placenta, a condition that can lead to life-threatening infection and blood loss.

After the surgery, I recovered well and began the task of adjusting to the challenges of new motherhood—without the wisdom I could have gotten from my mom and the other women in my life who had been through this already. I committed myself to being the perfect mom, and for me, that image included breastfeeding, but my son refused to play along with my vision for us. He quickly undid my image of mother and child surrounded by a halo of heavenly light as he blissfully and calmly received nourishment from my body. He never latched on. In fact, he was colicky and cried for hours upon hours. I was sleep deprived and somewhat delusional. The next few months required some serious adjustments, but eventually, we got the hang of it and got into a routine.

● ● ●

When I first arrived at the mother's program, there were only eight women living there, but over time it doubled to about sixteen. You can imagine how stressful it was for so many women to live together in one huge room, sharing one bathroom area, while dealing with the stresses of taking care of our infant children. Catty fights, attitudes, baby-daddy drama, cussing, fighting over the phone, and hormone-driven meltdowns filled our days. We even had several paternity dilemmas, situations in which a woman thought one man was the father of her baby and it turned out to be somebody else—like an episode of *Maury*. Lawd, help us all! Headphones and earplugs became my best friends.

Fortunately, I found Leslie, a woman my age who had a little girl, and we instantly clicked. Both business owners, spiritual, and laid-back, we found it easy to connect. We shared parenting tips, played Spades, talked about our plans, and really supported each other. Sometimes she cried on my shoulder, and other times I cried on hers. Leslie had an older son, so when I freaked out about small things as a first-time mom, she helped me remain calm. We spent so much time together that I always say her daughter was my son's first girlfriend. Leslie left a few months before I did, but she really helped quiet my nerves about dealing with a demanding baby, missing my family, and living with a bunch of hormonal women. Leslie and I are still really good friends.

During this time, I started a workout club so the other new mothers and I could all lose the baby weight, and I even started a small business class. I wanted to make sure I used my time wisely. I didn't want to become complacent or lazy. I wanted to be active, physically and mentally.

My husband and I talked and wrote often. I sent him lots of pictures of our new son, and he came to visit. Anthony was so proud of his baby boy. You could just see the love in his eyes when he stared at his son. It had to be very difficult for him to be separated from us, but he was the best father ever, making sure we both had everything we needed.

● ● ●

I stayed with my son in the program for eleven months. Then came the dreadful day when I had to take him home to my husband, leave him behind, and return to the camp to serve the rest of my sentence. Anthony arrived early in the morning to pick us up. I met him with our son, who I'd dressed in the cutest little baby-blue outfit, which my mother had bought him. It was winter and cold outside, but fortunately, the outfit had a matching hat, mittens, and throw blanket. My husband greeted me with the biggest hug and kiss. I said good-bye to everyone in the program, and we were on our way home.

The program allowed me a seven-day furlough to go home with my child and get him adjusted. When I arrived home, Anthony spent time bonding with our son, and my husband and I happily got reacquainted as well. My friends and family also came to visit and to get a glimpse of the new addition to our family. It was truly a time of celebration, good times, great food, and loving on one another.

Seven days went by so fast; it seemed like seven hours. The night before I was to return to the camp, I tossed and turned while my stomach did nervous flips. In just one week, I had settled back into the life I wanted with my family, and now it was going to end. Lying in bed, I saw all kinds of visions of how my son would feel without his mom and how my husband would have to manage raising our teenage daughter and young son all by himself. I felt regret, shame, and anger at myself for placing us in this position.

The morning of my departure, we got up early so I could be back at the camp by noon, the required time. I showered, prayed, cooked breakfast for us, and spent some time mentally preparing myself for the next year and a half. Anthony packed all my stuff, and we headed to my parents' house to drop off the baby. My mom and dad would keep our son while Anthony drove me back to the camp.

When it was time to go, I held my son with a fierce protectiveness, as if someone were trying to tear him from my arms. I didn't want to let him go, and I kissed and hugged him countless times. I told him how much his mommy loved him and that I was going to miss him so much. Anthony had to tell me several times, "Okay, baby. It's time to go." Finally, he pried me from our son and put me in the car. I was determined to be strong and not cry in front of our little boy. My eyes watered, but even though I was drowning with tears and sorrow on the inside, I didn't let a tear fall.

Anthony and I both tried to remain upbeat about my return to the camp. We focused on being thankful that I'd had the opportunity to raise our son for the first eleven months of his life, and I found some solace in the fact that Anthony would have time to really bond with and love on our son. That time would establish a strong relationship between them that would last their whole lives.

Our drive down to the facility was peaceful as we reminisced about all the fun we'd enjoyed over the last week, the many cute faces our son made, and the milestones he was reaching. As we arrived back at the camp, I knew the drill. Give my husband a kiss and a hug, check in, body search, bend over and cough, give everything to my husband, except my Bible, and get ready for round number two.

The first night away from my family was so hard for me. I'd gone from seeing our son every waking hour of the day and night (he still woke up at night to eat) and being with my husband for the last seven days to completely separated from both of them. I'd gone from a week in the comfort and privacy of our home to living in a cubicle-sized room with no door and an open ceiling, where everybody could see everything happening with me and around me.

That first night, I replayed the fun times my family and I had enjoyed over that short week. I didn't have any pictures from our time together yet because my husband had to mail them to me. I wasn't allowed to bring photos back with me, so I had to rely on my memories. As the hours ticked past, I stared at the ceiling, praying for strength to get through the night and the months to come. I cried, prayed, cried, prayed, and eventually got an hour or two of fitful sleep.

The entire experience of being away from my family for another year and a half would test my strength, will, faith, and endurance. It wasn't easy being separated from the people I loved most in the world, but that wasn't my biggest problem. At some point I had to face the reality that I was in prison. I had to deal with it, and I had to deal with me.

Denying what you feel will not make it go away. It ensures that it never gets resolved.

AUTHOR UNKNOWN

Chapter 17
Denial Doesn't Look Good on Me

During my three years in prison (even though the sentence was for forty-six months, I only served a portion of the time), I lived in denial. The few times I spoke about my prison experience with friends, I said I was on vacation or an extended retreat, at Bible College, or off on some other socially acceptable adventure. I avoided dealing with the realities of the situation because that denial helped my time go by faster.

I immersed myself in teaching, writing, learning, and exercising. I ghostwrote two books, developed small business curricula, taught Bible study, and stayed productive. I kept busy from the time I woke up until the time I went to bed. All this served me in the sense that it kept my mind focused. It hurt me in the sense that I wasn't dealing with my emotions.

I ignored or repressed the anger, resentment, unforgiveness of myself, and range of other challenging emotions that dwelled just below the surface of my smile. Little by little, many of the unresolved issues I had from my previous relationship spilled over into my marriage. I thought I'd handled them all in counseling, but they kept resurfacing, so obviously I had more work to do.

You would think I'd have been a very appreciative and loving wife because of my husband's support, the way he continued to show up for me, and the love and effort he was putting into raising our children while I was gone. Sometimes I was, but other times I was emotionally unstable, selfish, and downright confused. Worst of all, I didn't even realize it; I thought I was fine.

Sometimes my husband and I had the most loving conversations about how much we missed each other and what we would do when I got home, and other times not so much. I'd ramble on and on about what was happening in my day, what I needed, and how I wanted my son to be raised. I gave my opinion about potty training, how our child should eat, and his developing social skills. I wasn't sensitive to all my husband had going on in his life. Instead, I was caught up in being away from my family, missing my kids, being physically confined, dealing with raging hormones, and leaving behind the life I once knew.

Anthony had to be overwhelmed with working, raising our son and our teenage daughter (who lived with us full time), and performing the roles of a mother and father in my absence. It had to be difficult for my husband to be the primary caregiver of a two-year-old. While potty training our son, introducing him to shapes and colors, and making sure he got regular time to play outside, my husband was also solely responsible for our family's financial wellbeing.

That would be enough to stress anybody out. I had to learn I couldn't micro-manage what was happening at home when I was hundreds of miles away, but it wasn't an easy lesson for me to get. The time apart was so emotionally, mentally, and spiritually difficult for both of us. Anthony was trying to maintain the home front and also bring our kids to see me as often as possible. He had help from my parents and my brother, but the bulk of the responsibility fell on him.

In the midst of all this, my husband still did little special things that meant so much. One Valentine's Day, he sent me twelve cards in lieu of a dozen roses since you can't receive roses in prison. I was so touched by the gesture, which made me feel so special. During mail call, everyone waited in an open area, and the ladies would look on to see who got mail. To hear my name called twelve times was a special treat.

Even with those moments of relief and comfort to break up the monotony, I struggled. I was so emotional every time my family came to visit, especially my husband and kids. I'd see them for a few hours in visitation, knowing I couldn't go back home with them, but instead of giving in to and expressing how that made me feel. I protected myself by becoming somewhat emotionally detached so it wouldn't hurt so badly. I was physically present, but not one hundred percent mentally and emotionally present. After a while that catches up with you, and you become desensitized.

In retrospect, my husband and I both believe the fact that I was pregnant and gave birth to our older son during this time was a blessing in disguise (as my father always says). I was so focused on my son during the first year that I didn't have time to concentrate on the realities of life in prison. Anthony was so focused on making sure we had everything we needed that he didn't have time to think about anything else. Those years were truly a roller-coaster ride for us both. Fortunately, all "good things" come to an end, and the time finally came to say goodbye to the camp and start the next chapter in my life.

Saying goodbye isn't the hard part; it's what we leave behind that's tough.

AUTHOR UNKNOWN

Chapter 18
Saying Goodbye Is Bittersweet

Without a shadow of a doubt, purpose was birthed in me during my stay at the camp. At the point when you have nothing to depend on but God, He can really start to deal with you. That's why so many people don't find their way until they hit rock bottom, and that was definitely true for me.

In the camp, I didn't have luxury cars, designer clothes, or shoes and bags to distract me. There was nobody to impress. I was on my own with my thoughts and feelings. Previously, I had pursued other people's dreams and chased after money. Finally, my life became all about finding my passion and God's purpose for me.

Everything had happened in my life for a reason. I realized this even while I was still in the middle of dealing with the consequences of my choices. Before my arrest, God had been whispering to me, telling me I was going down the wrong path, but I hadn't listened. God started off speaking quietly, then His voice got a bit louder, and finally I got hit with a Mack truck that knocked me flat out. Once I was in a position where I had to listen, I was able to reflect on my choices through a lens of honesty and growing self-awareness.

During my relationship with Kent, my mom had dreamed she saw me in a police car. After the dream, she tried to warn me. "I have no idea what you're doing," she said, "but my dreams have meaning." I talked to Kent about it, but he blew it off, and I let it go. In so many instances over the decade we were together, I knew I was supposed to make a different decision, but I didn't. Going to the prison camp was God's way of screaming at me because I didn't listen to the whispers, like my mother's dream.

While I was with Kent, I also ignored God's calling on my life, setting aside my passion so I could support his. From an early age, I'd had a passion for motivating women. It didn't matter what you were going through, I was going to give you a positive word and uplift your spirit while we were talking. I hated to see people hurt and wanted to help every woman I crossed paths with have a better life. I wanted to be a motivational speaker or coach even before I really knew what those jobs were. I loved empowering women to have a better life, but I'd let all that go so I could help Kent get what he wanted.

While I served my time, officials could have given me any job on the campus, from cooking to working in commissary or landscaping, but God worked it out and gave me a coveted role in the education department. I was open to working any job they gave me—not that I had a choice—but after just a few days in the education department, I knew my assignment was God ordained. I started off teaching one class and, over time, taught almost every class, including health, small business, career development, and personal finance.

In essence, I ran the education department, but I remained humble and dared not hint at that to my boss, who complimented me often on how easy I made her job. One day, she said, "You would be an amazing executive assistant. You're so organized." While there are powerhouse women and men in that role, and they're often the ones keeping the C-suite functioning effectively, my boss didn't know me at all. I thought, *Lady, I ran million-dollar businesses. Don't get it twisted.* But I liked my job, so I smiled and said, "Thank you so much. What a nice compliment."

● ○ ●

In a career development class I taught, three ladies stood out to me. One was a very attractive Black woman with a slender build. Five-eight with long, light-brown hair, she could easily have been a Cover Girl model. During class, she shared, "I've been a stripper since I was eighteen, and I'm twenty-five now. All I know how to do is entice men with my body for money."

After she spoke, a white woman in her mid-forties said, "All I know how to do is to sell drugs." Drugs, she explained, were her family business. Her father had gone to prison, and several of her siblings were in and out of prison too.

Then a white woman in her early thirties, a self-described trust fund baby, stood to speak. Her parents were very wealthy and spoiled her rotten. She had gotten caught up in an illegal medical scam with her husband, and her parents had disowned them.

All these ladies had one thing in common. The lifestyle they had known would not be available to them when they were released. Their candidness surprised me, and I listened attentively as each told her story. When they were done, I said, "Listen, ladies. You have transferable skills. You know logistics and distribution, supply and demand, customer service, marketing, operations, finance, and a host of other skills. All you have to do is change the product you're selling. Instead of selling drugs, your body, or a fantasy, you can sell a real, tangible, and legal product or service." I went on to say, "You have everything within you to be great and successful. Don't let your past define you. Use what you know as a stepping-stone, and build from that."

To see those ladies' faces light up was priceless. Most of the women in the class said no one had ever believed in them. Instead, they'd been told they were worthless and would never become anything. The encouraging message I shared with them hadn't come from me, however. It had come through me. The words out of my mouth were giving those ladies hope, but I couldn't take the credit. This type of occurrence became my new normal.

● ● ●

When I started a Bible study, more than fifty ladies attended the first session. At my request, everyone brought a pocket-size mirror and stared themselves directly in the eyes. Then we did an exercise in which I asked them to say three positive words to describe themselves. Many of the women stared blankly in the mirror because they had no positive words to say about the woman they saw reflected there. Others described themselves with terms like giving, great mother, or loving wife.

As they went on, I noticed most of the women listed external characteristics, based on what they did for others, as their positive attributes. Few identified internal traits based on who they were. This powerful exercise awakened something in them because, as most of us do, they'd spent a lifetime looking through themselves, never really looking deep into themselves. Tears flowed, and women realized things about themselves that they had never verbalized. It was freeing and scary at the same time. I was nervous because I didn't want to take these ladies somewhere I couldn't bring them back from, but God was faithful and led us all through this self-discovery exercise.

I spent hours studying the Bible, a concordance, and everything I could get my hands on that might be helpful. My husband, family, and friends must have grown tired of me asking them to Google stuff for me and receiving wish lists of books to buy me, but I used that knowledge to create programs and pour everything I had into those ladies. I mentored, counseled, prayed, drafted resumes, helped write business plans, and did anything I could to ensure they each had the best possible start when they left the camp.

I even started a marriage-focused Bible study and taught on the role of a wife, which included teaching submission of a wife to her husband. I was—and still am—a very independent, strong-willed woman, so God had to do a lot of work with me to even prepare me to deliver this message. My views on submission evolved to a deeper understanding that submission is protection and covering. Your husband is submitted to God's direction for your family, and you are submitted to your husband unto God. It's like God is the umbrella your husband is holding and you're under the umbrella with your husband to protect you from getting wet.

I also grew to understand that you submit to each other's strengths. For example, my husband submits to my strengths in handling our kids schooling, and I submit to his strengths about managing our household finances. This is a long way from my initial thoughts, which we don't even need to discuss. Let's just say I've come a long way.

Now, if *my* views had to change significantly, you can imagine how the first class went as I tried to teach a group of women—many of whom had experienced toxic relationships with men—that God wanted them to submit to a man. Strong opinions, attitudes, and cries of "I don't want to hear it" filled the room. However, after six weeks of learning and growing together, I believe marriages were strengthened and old views were replaced with love and dedication to being a godly wife.

This time of preparation was so valuable for me. God removed outside distractions and gave me time to focus on Him and hone my craft. The programs I teach today are based on my life experiences and much of the information I learned during this three-year period.

● ○ ●

One Saturday afternoon, I was reading in the recreation yard when God sent me an angel in the body of a petite Hispanic woman who prophesied over me about God's plan for my life. She said I would teach women about being good wives and mothers. She told me God was going to use my business experience, but my role wasn't teaching about business. She encouraged me to be bold and step out in what God was telling me to do. She also taught me about submitting to God's will and not getting caught up in what I saw or thought I wanted or needed in life. To this day, she has no idea of the positive impact she had on me and my destiny. This message so spoke to my spirit and confirmed what God was telling me.

As my time at the camp neared its end, I was so excited to get back home, but leaving the new family I had made was also bittersweet. I would miss pouring into the ladies' lives and getting filled with the knowledge that I was planting just a small seed that would be watered by others and later spring up into a wonderful harvest. I missed my family and was ready to go home, but God surely did fill me with the work He had me do at the camp. With 1,095 days behind me, it was time for me to leave and reunite with my family. My sentence was over, but my transition would present new challenges.

Love begins at home, and it is not how much we do, but how much love we put in that action.

MOTHER TERESA

Chapter 19
Wife and Mom at Home

The day finally came when the doors opened for me to walk out of the facility. Filled with excitement about going home and being reunited with my family, I woke up extra early that morning. I went to the office to be processed for release and changed into the street clothes my husband had mailed in for me. Stepping into jeans and pulling on a t-shirt felt like heaven.

Most ladies would get all dressed up with stilettos and fancy dresses for their release. However, I wasn't going straight home. I had to live in a halfway house for a few months first, so I chose comfort over cuteness. It was time for me to roll my sleeves up and work. I had to find a job, show steady income, and make sure I had good ties to the community before I would be fully released to go home.

After I was dressed, the staff officer told me my husband was there. She looked through all my boxes, searched me to make sure I wasn't taking anything from the camp, and had me fill out my release paperwork. Then she escorted me to the door, where I was surprised to see my boss from the education department waiting for me. She explained that she wanted to meet the wonderful man I often spoke about so highly.

When I saw my husband standing there in his jeans, button-down shirt, and casual loafers, my heart dropped. He looked as handsome as ever, and I fell in love all over again. I was hoping my boss would hurry up and finish talking so I could just eat Anthony up. When we finally made it to the car, I locked lips with him for at least five minutes and didn't want to let go. I was so happy to be back in his arms.

I only had a few hours to make it to the halfway house, so Anthony and I were pushing it for time. I wanted to go by and see family and friends, but we had to head straight to my temporary residence. We picked up a quick bite to eat at a drive-through and then lugged my belongings into the admissions area of the halfway house. Other people were arriving and checking in at the same time, so we had to wait for a while before I was processed. Fortunately, that gave us a little more time to talk and hang out.

My homecoming was very low-key, which was fine with us. My husband and I had agreed he wouldn't bring our son because we didn't want our first mother-son interaction to be dropping me off and separating right away. We wanted my reunion with our son to happen when I would have more time to spend with him.

I spent the first week at the halfway house getting settled in and immediately finding a job. I needed to receive at least two paychecks before I would be granted a weekend pass to go home. Thankfully, a family friend, who ran a nonprofit agency, gave me a job, and I would be able to start going home within the first month.

In the meantime, my parents came to visit. Our daughter had moved back in with her mom to finish her senior year, but my husband brought our son to see me, and when I saw my little boy, my heart opened. He gave me the biggest hug and kisses, and I just melted. I loved on him during the entire visit except when he wanted to get down and play. We had such a good time spending quality family time together.

●　●　●

After living at the halfway house for months, I was finally released to go home. Still keeping my transition to normal life fairly private, Anthony and I decided we wanted to get settled in our new home before we had an official homecoming with family and friends. We needed to get reacquainted with each other and find our rhythm before anything else. It wasn't like we'd lived together for a long time or gotten to know each other's ways before I left. We'd only been married a little over six months before we were forced to live apart from each other, so this was very new for us.

Anthony had moved our family into a new house while I was away, so I had to make myself comfortable in a new environment. I also had to bond again with our son, learn his personality, and try to get settled in a new career and business. This period was filled with frustration and many mis-understandings balanced with lots of grace and love from my husband.

One of the hardest things Anthony had to deal with in our marriage was my transition back into my freedom. I'd been told the length of time you were away was how long it would take you to readjust. If you'd been away for three years, for example, it would take you approximately three years to fit comfortably back into your normal life. Initially, I didn't believe it could take that long, but as I was readjusting to our mar-riage and family life, I found the estimation had merit. I was one person when I left and someone else when I returned be-cause, in some ways, I had been shaped by my experiences and environment. The same went for my husband. He had de-veloped routines for how he ran the household and dealt with the children. He had to make room for me, and I had to come in and figure out where my place was in all of it.

For most of my life, I had suppressed my feelings. I was always the person to solve everybody else's problems. I was the one who was always positive, regardless of the situation. When I went to prison, it was no different. I helped start a wom-en's ministry, taught business and life skills classes, coached people, and focused on everyone else. I was finding my pur-pose, yes, but I didn't deal with my real feelings and the reality of my situation.

Because of that, when I came home, I was in a mental space of wanting to do me. I had always done what everybody else wanted me to do, for my entire life, and now it was my turn. I had done what my parents wanted, then my ex-boy-friend, then the government, and *here we go again*, I thought, with my husband. How many of you know "doing me" doesn't work when you're a wife and a mother, especially when your husband has stood by you for three years, while you were away, and raised your children?

My mentality was so backwards when I came home. I wanted to start my business again, right away, and focus on building an empire. Putting my financial trust in someone and having it ripped apart had left me so scarred that I wanted to do whatever I could to make sure it didn't happen again. I felt like I had to build up my savings to ensure I could always take care of myself.

I should have been making sure my family was healthy in every way before worrying about business, but I had my priorities mixed up. Now, don't get me wrong. I was there as a mother and wife, but I wasn't as mentally and emotionally present as I should have been. I had been defined by my business and my accomplishments for my entire life. Growing up, I was a high-achiever and started my first company at nine-teen. Hard work and commitment to my business were what I knew, so I instinctively dove into those things.

When I came home and got a job making $8.00 an hour as an executive assistant, I didn't know how to adjust to what felt like a fall from where I'd once been. It took me a long time to be okay with earning so much less than I was accustomed to making. My frustration with the dramatic drop in salary and my desire to do something different caused a huge strain on my marriage.

Anthony believed I should focus on rebuilding our family and marriage. He was absolutely right, but I wasn't there yet. I used the words "my" and "I" a lot, instead of "our" and "we." I lost sight of the fact that this time was about our family transitioning together, not just me transitioning home.

Life got better, however, and I went from $8.00 an hour to a part-time organizational development and change management consulting position at $1,750 per month within the first year. Within two years, I started doing contracting training and leadership development work at $6,600 per month, and finally, I had my own business within four years. I was on a roll. Now that my money was right, it was time to expand.

You will either step forward into growth, or you will step backward into safety.

ABRAHAM MASLOW

Chapter 20
It's Time to Expand

During our transition period, our marriage had ups and downs—high highs and low lows—and two significantly affected our relationship. First, my husband decided he wanted to try his hand at entrepreneurship. He'd always had a passion for mentoring young men and wanted to launch a non-profit organization teaching decision-making skills to at-risk youth.

My husband didn't grow up with his father, and he was determined to break this cycle in our family. Because of his experience, he worked hard to learn and grow in the area of fatherhood. He provided his children with everything he didn't have as a child. He was emotionally present and physically available, and he loved them with everything inside him. My husband also had a real gift for reading people and speaking into their lives. For all these reasons, I believed he was perfectly made for the mentoring work he felt called to do.

True to his nature for building and growing as a family, Anthony asked me to help him with the business, but I was less than excited about the idea. In fact, I wondered how he could ask me for my help when I'd just spent three years in prison for choices I'd made while helping a man start and build his business. I had zero interest in getting involved in my husband's business in any way.

I hadn't forgotten about the three years *my husband*, not just some man, stood by me, but even after all he'd done for me, I wasn't ready to go down that road just yet. I didn't realize it, but I was still traumatized from the whole experience with Kent and our legal problems. Don't misunderstand me. I was extremely happy for my husband and supported what he wanted to do. I even gave him several ideas and suggestions. I brainstormed with him and wrote out some of the curriculum for a pilot program. I just wasn't in a mental space to build a business with him when I was trying to figure out who I was, how to fill my demanding roles as wife and mother, and how to find my place in society once again.

My reluctance had a huge negative impact on my husband, some of which he verbalized. At the heart of it all, it made him feel like I lacked gratitude and appreciation for all he'd done for me while I was away. Anthony wanted to build a legacy for our family. He was doing it all for us. I, on the other hand, was still dealing with where I'd just come from, and I wasn't ready to venture down that path with him. I wasn't saying I'd never be ready to help with the business, but it was way too soon for me.

It sometimes seemed like my husband thought I'd been on vacation, relaxing and chilling, like life in the camp was a day at the beach. He couldn't possibly understand the profound mental and emotional effect serving that sentence had on me. No, I wasn't in a maximum-security prison made up of tiny cells, each with a single toilet shared among many residents, but I'd been snatched away from my family. I'd done exactly what I was told, day in and day out. I'd adhered to specific hours to get up and go to bed. I'd eaten what I was given. I'd been referred to as a number and often looked at as less than a human. Decisions about my life had been made by other people, and I'd had no ability to exercise my free will. Worst of all, I couldn't leave. At home with my family, I was trying to put all the pieces together and recover from that experience.

The second momentous event that affected our marriage was our decision to expand our family. I was so happy to find out I was pregnant again. The home test was positive, but when I went to the doctor for my first check-up, something was wrong. The ultrasound showed I was about eight-weeks pregnant, but the baby was measuring at six weeks, and they couldn't find a heartbeat. I was devastated when the doctor told me I was having a miscarriage.

My body went through the natural process of miscarrying, but I was numb. I really didn't say much to my husband about it. Instead, I suffered in silence. I wanted another child, so we continued to try, and within a short period of time, I was pregnant again. Again, I was excited and overjoyed. I went to the doctor for my first appointment, and they did all the blood work and confirmed my pregnancy.

A few weeks later, my mom accompanied me for the ultrasound. This time, the doctor looked back and forth from the screen to my stomach with a puzzled look on his face. After a few minutes, he told me that even though I was eight or nine weeks pregnant, the baby was only measuring at six weeks. I was miscarrying again. My mom didn't know what to say, and I said nothing.

Within a six-month period, I'd had two miscarriages. Devastated and drained, I questioned my womanhood and whether I would ever be able to have more children. The doctor had me come back in for a follow-up visit to test my hormone levels, after which he assured me miscarriages were normal and I could still carry a healthy baby.

Anthony and I didn't talk much about what happened. He tried to comfort and support me, and I appreciated his efforts, but this was something I had to deal with in my own way. The miscarriages were rough for me, and the pain was made worse because I didn't talk about them. I kept my feelings to myself and hoped I'd get pregnant again and carry a healthy baby to term.

I did my best to process the pain internally, but for a while, every time I saw a pregnant woman, I broke out in tears. I found it difficult to go to the doctor for follow-up appointments because every time I did, someone in the waiting room was pregnant. It seemed like women who didn't even want kids were getting pregnant and popping out healthy babies—one, two, three—with no effort.

I allowed myself to have a pity party and wondered if I was being punished for bad decisions I'd made in my life. I also worried about how the miscarriages might affect our marriage. How did my husband feel since I hadn't been able to give him more kids? Did he blame me? Was it my fault? I felt guilty, and I felt like a failure.

I didn't know how to deal with these losses. I didn't want to go to any support groups. I didn't want to mourn the loss of my unborn children. Finally, I talked to my good friend, who had experienced three miscarriages, and she provided me with great comfort and hope because she'd gone on to have three healthy and beautiful children. She suggested I take it one day at a time. I would mourn my losses sooner or later, she explained, but in my own time. She told me that years after they'd happened, she'd break down crying while watching something on TV that made her think of the miscarriages she suffered. Like me, she hadn't been able to deal with them when they first occurred.

As we talked about our experiences, my friend told me she didn't understand how I could go to prison, remain positive, and come home and slide right back into my life. I told her I didn't understand how she could go through three miscarriages and still remain positive and hopeful throughout the process of trying to grow her family. In the past, I never could have imagined going through one miscarriage, let alone two, but you never really know what you can bear until you go through it.

I prayed a lot and read Scriptures about multiplying and my seed being blessed. I gave my body time to rest, and months later, I missed my period. I was a little scared to take the test, but I did, and it was positive. I waited a while before I went in for my check-up, though I did start taking my prenatal vitamins. At the doctor's office, they did all the blood work and my first ultrasound. Praise God! We heard a heartbeat.

Cautious and a bit afraid, I didn't allow myself to get excited about this pregnancy until I was almost seven months along because I wanted to make sure I wasn't going to experience another disappointment. I just knew in my heart of hearts that it was a little girl, but it turned out we were having another boy. My husband was elated. I'd always wanted a girl, but God had blessed me with an older daughter, and now it was round number two for boys.

Once I shared the good news, my mother and my closest girlfriends went into overdrive planning the baby shower. My mother had already demonstrated her skills when she gave me my dream wedding. And as the queen of event planning, she would make sure my baby shower was just as enjoyable and memorable.

My baby shower was an amazing day filled with games, dancing, good food, and laughter. As big as a house, I still hit the dance floor, doing the Wobble and the Electric Side. I even tried to drop it like it was hot, got stuck on the floor, and needed help to get back up. I guess I forgot I was carrying around an extra sixty pounds.

Anthony was thrilled about having another boy, and our son was incredibly excited to become a big brother. I started to prepare myself for sleep deprivation, dirty diapers, breast-feeding, and a bit of chaos—but this time, with all hands on deck.

Priorities: When someone tells you they are too "busy," it's not a reflection of their schedule; it's a reflection of your spot on their schedule.

STEVE MARABOLI

Chapter 21
The Rubber Meets the Road

Anyone who has ever said building a business with a baby on your hip and a toddler on your leg, while cooking, cleaning, and pleasing a husband was easy needs to be checked. As most parents of infants know, when there's a newborn in the house, the added strain magnifies any problems in your marriage. I don't know if it's the sleep deprivation, hormonal changes, lack of attention and lack of sex, or all the above. Regardless of the causes, this is when the rubber meets the road.

Imagine you're trying to breastfeed, and your infant son is barely latching on, you need to make sure your older child has everything he needs for pre-K4, your husband is asking you to consider getting a job and put your business on hold for a while once you're ready to work, and you feel like you haven't slept in days. All you want is to take a shower, but five minutes alone in the bathroom would suffice. That was my life after our second son came into the world, and at times I wondered if I was about to have a breakdown or if I was just overwhelmed in the ways many new mothers are.

The days leading up to my delivery had been very relaxed. I finished a contract and took off several weeks from my business. However, once our bundle of joy arrived, life became chaotic. Building a business places great demands on time and resources, so I wanted to take some time off to really focus on the baby and get our older son adjusted to the new addition to the family. I also needed time to work with my husband to acclimate our marriage to the needs of a new baby. I didn't realize, however, that adjustment period at home all day with our son was going to be a lot shorter than I expected.

● ● ●

After four months at home with the baby, I received a phone call about a consulting project. It was a unique opportunity that would afford me lots of flexibility to run my business on a small scale and give me time to provide my family with everything they needed from me. I had a wonderful family friend who ran an in-home day care, and I knew she would love my son as her own. So I was off on my next business adventure, ready to conquer the world.

Being the "shero" I wanted to be came at a huge price. Fast forward a year or so, and the foundation of my marriage had started to shake. From the outside looking in, everything seemed to be going great. Our marriage was stable, the children were taken care of, and life was good. But lots of families look perfect in family portraits. You never know what's going on behind those smiles.

Just as in any marriage, we had ups and downs. There were things we agreed upon and other things about which we agreed to disagree. One of the latter was my business. From the time I returned home from Florida, I was so focused on building the business that often—well, let's just be real—most times, I placed work above my family.

Anthony talked with me many times about balancing my business and our family. He told me my priorities were off and family had to come first. I heard him with my ears, but I didn't take to heart what he was saying. I'd nod my head in agreement, and then I'd keep right on doing things my way. My husband isn't one to just keep talking; he's ex-military and believes in taking action. True to his nature, he finally sat me down for a fateful conversation.

One Friday morning, while I was working in my home office, Anthony came in and said, "Honey, we need to talk." Yes, he said those words women dread hearing just as much as men do. He continued, "I love you with all my heart, but I don't know how to get through to you. I feel like your business consumes you, and all the kids and I get are your leftovers. I've been asking you for years to restructure your priorities and give us more of you. I've been asking you for years to help and support me in the way that I need. I'm drained," he said, "and I don't have anything else left in me to keep giving to you and not receiving. I've thought long and hard about this, and if things don't change, I can't continue on this way. I'll want a divorce."

Wait a minute. Did he just use the d-word?

If I had really been listening to him over all those months, his words wouldn't have shocked me. As it was, they caught me off guard. A sense of panic swept over me, and I fought to hold back my tears when I really wanted to break down and cry. The word *divorce* was forbidden in our house. Once we were married, that was it. Our marriage was for life.

I'd never heard my husband talk like that, not once, regardless of what we'd gone through, even when I was locked away in the federal facility. But Anthony had finally reached his breaking point. For years, he gave and gave and never felt like his needs were met. He probably resented that I hadn't come home from prison and jumped into a role as doting wife and mother who put her family before anything else. As I listened to his ultimatum, I thought about my selfishness, my ungratefulness, and all the ways I must have disappointed him.

I asked my husband to tell me exactly what he wasn't receiving in our marriage and how I could change. Anthony didn't hold back. He gave me a laundry list that could fill this book, and I was left wondering if I had ever done anything right.

For the sake of space and keeping some of my business to myself, I'll just give you a few highlights from my husband's complaints.

One, I'm tired of you coming to bed every night with your bonnet on. Yes, ladies, I said it. The dreaded, non-sexy bonnet—that was me most nights.

Two, by the end of the day, you're exhausted, but if your phone rings with a new client, you're out of the bed and on the computer. He was right. It was amazing how I had energy for the things I really wanted to do.

Three, everything is about work with you. You're on the computer late at night, emailing when you're supposed to be spending time with the kids, going to way too many week-end events, and not spending quality time with your family. Obviously, my priorities were out of order.

Four, you're so busy handling your business, motivating everybody else, and saving the world that you fail to see how much more of you your family needs. That was so true, nothing left to say.

Five, you're disrespectful. I didn't really understand how he could say I disrespected him until he broke it down for me. Anthony asked if I respected him, why didn't I do the things he asked me to do? Why did we always have to argue about it? He explained that if I respected him, then I should trust his judgment and know he wouldn't do anything to harm our family.

Five points are enough. You get the picture. After a two-hour conversation, I really couldn't say anything except, "You are absolutely right."

In reflecting on our conversation, I recalled times when my older son would say: "Mommy, when are you going to be finished on the computer? Mommy, why are you checking e-mail while we're supposed to be playing? Mommy, can you go on this field trip with me?" But I'd keep working or miss the field trip because I had a client to serve.

I thought back to times when my husband had said to me: "I'm not your ex-boyfriend. Stop trying to make me pay for what he did to you. I love you, I'm here for you, and I'm not going anywhere. I would never intentionally hurt you. Stop trying to sabotage our marriage, and let me love you."

Whew, child! Emotional baggage is no joke, especially, when you don't realize you're still carrying it. I had no idea these deep-rooted issues were still there and affecting my marriage. In essence, I had no idea what a healthy relationship looked like. I had become so accustomed to dysfunction that I was unintentionally sabotaging my marriage because I didn't know how to properly handle my husband's love. I was so busy listening to the latest business podcast or coming up with ideas for my next program that I was letting my marriage slip through my fingers.

I also realized my husband's love language was acts of service and mine was words of affirmation. So when I was saying positive words and complimenting him, I wasn't doing anything to build him up. He needed to see my love in action instead of just hearing about it. (If you haven't read *The Five Love Languages*, by Gary Chapman, I encourage you to get a copy today. It saved me a lot of heartache in my marriage and helped me understand how differently my husband and I communicate our love to one another.)

Since my husband's love language was acts of service, he felt loved when I did what he asked me do for him. Acts of service like cooking, washing dishes, or doing laundry weren't filling up his love tank because I'd do those things anyway. More than that, he needed me to cooperate when he asked me to do something for the kids, handle some business for him, or do other things that are a little too personal to share (but you get the idea).

I thought I was rocking and rolling as a wife and mother, making sure laundry was done, everyone was fed, the house was cleaned, and the kids had what they needed. What more did my husband need? Apparently, a lot more.

We were on two different pages as far as what made us feel loved. My husband was a provider and protector. He thought making sure the bills were paid and coming home every night would make me feel loved. Since I needed words of affirmation, all his acts of service failed to register as love to me. Yes, I appreciated that he put gas in the car and ensured everything at home was taken care of. However, I needed to hear him say, "I love you, I'm proud of you, and you're doing a great job with the kids." In his mind, being there equaled "I love you."

I often found myself so caught up in business that, as long as the basics were covered, I didn't take the time to do the little extra things. You know the basics; the kids are breathing, and there's no blood. If that was the case, I was good to go. Too often, I was present physically, but not mentally or emotionally.

After Anthony gave me that ultimatum, I realized I didn't want life to pass me by. I didn't want to wake up one morning and discover my kids were grown and I didn't have a relationship with them. I didn't want my husband and me to look at each other when our kids were eighteen and moving out, and realize we didn't have a relationship because everything had been about the kids and work.

For a long time, I thought my husband didn't support my business, but he helped me understand what he didn't support was *the way* I was doing business. He supported my business one hundred percent, he explained, but our family should always come first. He suggested that once our family had everything they needed, I could absolutely go hard for my business. The problem was my family wasn't getting the best part of me, and I wasn't making the necessary adjustments to organize my time and shift my priorities. I was going hard for my business one hundred percent but only giving my family fifty percent effort.

I learned many important lessons through this conversation and the work that followed. Three of those lessons stick out as the most impactful. First, you cannot give what you don't have. When I came home, my husband expected me to fall right into the role of being a wife and mother. He had a traditional vision of what that would look like. The problem was I didn't know who the heck I was. I couldn't step into the roles he wanted me to fill because I was still trying to define who I was and what I wanted for my life. It's very difficult to go through the self-discovery process when you're married with children. Your spouse and children have needs, wants, and desires they expect you to fulfill. However, if you are an empty vessel, you can't pour into anyone else.

If I could go back and do things differently, I wouldn't have made false and empty promises to my husband and myself. I would have continued going to counseling and worked through past issues to set myself on a journey to great success. It's difficult to work things out in your own head. Dealing with deeper issues, including the baggage most of us bring from childhood, usually requires the help of a coach, counselor, or friend.

Second, God has to be in control of your marriage and your life. I know without a shadow of a doubt that if God wasn't the head of my life and my husband's life, we would be divorced, and I would be a single parent. I was so out of order, for many years, in my marriage. I was disrespectful (most times without knowing it) and really selfish (not recognizing that either). I'm not a confrontational person, so when I admit to being disrespectful, I'm not talking about yelling, cursing, and fighting. I'm talking about not listening to what my husband needed and not providing it.

I was so focused on me that I couldn't hear what my husband was saying. My priorities were business, my children, and business again, and my husband had a place somewhere down the list. I wasn't even on the list. Given a second chance, I would reorder my priorities from the beginning to look like this: myself (my relationship with God and my self-care), my husband, my children, and then the business—in that order.

I should have prayed more and trusted God more. I should have listened more and talked less. It took me a while to realize I'd rather be happy than right. Simply put, I don't always have to say something. Silence can be golden. Most importantly, I should have let go and let God. I shouldn't have tried to push so hard with my business. Instead, I should have trusted God's timing for what He wanted to do with my family and business, and I should have been more patient.

Third, a wife must respect her husband and build him up. How can I expect my husband to love and adore me if I disrespect him and fail to build him up? I wish I would have truly gotten this lesson ten years earlier. I was tearing my husband down without even realizing it. The words that came out of my mouth and my actions, or better yet my inaction, had a tremendous effect on my husband. They cut him like a knife at his core.

Because I'm very assertive in business matters, I was so tapped into my masculine energy that I was bringing that energy home and not stepping into my femininity. Rather than complementing my husband, I behaved like I was competing with him. I had to learn that my individual goals could not conflict with the vision my husband had for our family. If I won and my husband or our children lost, then our team still lost. I had to shift my mind from focusing solely on my goals to focus on the higher vision for our family.

One important component of this change in priorities was making sure my husband's needs were met and realizing that I'm the helpmeet and not the leader of our family. I was expecting my husband to adjust to me because I didn't want to adjust to him. I wanted to do everything how and when I wanted to do it. Understanding this lesson was a sobering process. In fact, I'm still a work in progress in this area. If I could wave my magic wand and go back and change some things, I would be more submissive and cooperative with my husband. Yes, I said it, *more submissive*.

Since my husband is a man of God and has a great heart for his family, I would listen to him more and let him lead our family without resistance. I would give my input. However, if he made decisions for our family that I didn't agree with, I wouldn't fight him on them. I would just pray about it. I've learned that if I give it to God, it will always work out just like it's supposed to, even if I don't get what I want.

I've also learned that when I'm in a place of submission to my husband, he's submissive to me in my areas of strength. The Bible says, "Submit yourselves one to another." Since I'm strong in business, that's an area in which he can defer to me, just as I defer to his strengths. However, if I am out of order and not being a helpmeet, then our house and family are out of order. Before you get your panties in a tight wad, you should know my life and business always experience the most success when I'm in alignment with my family and my marriage. When I honor those things God has blessed me with in my life, He honors and blesses everything my hands touch. Do it, and see what happens.

While I can see all this now, I didn't receive these revelations overnight. I didn't become a new woman on the day my husband told me things needed to change between us, or he'd have to get a divorce. While I made some changes, I also had moments, over the following years, when I slid back into old ways of thinking and behaving, and our marriage suffered for it.

● ● ●

My husband also learned some lessons through this process, including these top three. One, don't allow someone else's words to affect the destiny of your life—even if that someone is your wife. Two, let God have a presence in your life and marriage. Don't immediately react based on your initial emotions because reacting to your initial emotions rarely leads to the best decision. Three, when you are a husband and father, even when you don't feel like it, you have to place the wellbeing of your family above what you want to do.

After reflecting on everything that had happened in my marriage and family, I knew it was time for me to make drastic changes in my life. God had given me this great man, and I was messing up big time. What was the point of having a great business I loved if I couldn't share it with my family? I truly wanted it all, and that included a husband and family who would share in the benefits of my successful business. My evolution continued.

How does one become a butterfly?
You must want to fly so much that
you are willing to give up being a
caterpillar.

TRINA PAULUS

Chapter 22
Woman Evolving

I used to think of my life in terms of a metamorphosis, as if I'd gone into a cocoon and come out a different person. In some ways, that's true. Yet, I've gone into that cocoon, for short or long periods, for small or large transformations, many times over. I went into that cocoon after my arrest, and when I went to prison, and when my husband gave me his ultimatum. Each time, I was changed in new ways, and I now realize that transformation never ends. Instead of going through a single metamorphosis, I am, in fact, ever evolving. Each stage of my life, the good and the bad, has brought me to a new level of maturity and closer to my God-ordained purpose. It's an ongoing process, not a one-time shift.

At one point, I put myself in solitary confinement for six months. I gave up social media (all the beautiful images and motivational quotes on my business page and in my group were posted by my social media expert at the time, my brother), and I focused on hearing God's direction. I only serviced the clients I already had, and in the rest of my time, I sat with God. It was such a surreal experience to block out every other voice, including my own, and listen to God's voice.

God was showing me the real me, and what I saw wasn't very pretty. He revealed the many areas in which I'd been disobedient in my marriage, in my role as a mother, and as a business owner. He showed me my shortcomings as a daughter, sister, and friend. This wasn't a rosy picture. During this time, God humbled me and stripped me of what I thought I wanted for my life, and He filled me with His grace and His purpose for me.

God started dealing with me—my insecurities, fears, doubts, lack of patience, shame, and guilt. He allowed me to see areas in my life where I trusted my own ability more than His. He showed me how to trust Him for my provision and look to Him for answers.

I finally had a true awakening and realized it was not my responsibility to make anybody else happy. I went on a journey to find out what made me truly happy. For years, I had placed other people's happiness above my own. Trying to live up to the image and expectations other people had of me had exhausted me. Living a life that wasn't authentic to me, pretending to be someone I wasn't, had been a daily struggle.

After her passing, I read an article about Whitney Houston on EUR WEB, a popular blogsite. The article included a quote from an anonymous record executive, who stated, "She was in pain from all the pressure she was facing and the pain from living almost a double life." After Clive Davis signed her to his label in 1985, the executive said, "She had to do what he said, wear what he said to, sing what he wanted her to sing, and act like a goody two shoes when she was really a down and dirty girl from Jersey. Whitney definitely resented that; she did drugs to escape her pain."

I didn't know Whitney Houston beyond her public image, but I related to the pain of living a lie. I'd lost the essence of who I truly was. She'd used drugs to cope with that pain. Some people escape with alcohol, sex, shopping, cigarettes, and a host of other numbing mechanisms. Sleeping and the emotional eating of strawberry shortcake and macaroni and cheese let me escape when I couldn't stand the pressure anymore.

I can't imagine the pressures Whitney must have felt every day, living her life under a microscope. On a small scale in my own life, even without the cameras and paparazzi with which she had to contend, I struggled. Stress ate at the core of who I was, and I lost a piece of myself every day.

Determined to finally live a life authentic to me, I had to take some time out to really discover who I was and what I wanted in my life. I had to reintroduce myself to me and reclaim my own worth. I had to remove the labels of wife, mom, business owner, daughter, and sister. I had to stop placing what everybody else wanted for me and from me above my own desires. I had to really dig deep to find out what I wanted for myself and be okay with it, regardless of what others thought.

I had to understand I was enough. Without the titles or the business, I was simply enough in my own skin. I was enough.

Whether I had a successful business or not, whether my kids were honor roll students or not, whether I was always a great wife or not, whether my house was clean or not, I was simply enough. I had to realize I was valuable and worthy in God's eyes, and therefore I was valuable and worthy to myself. It didn't matter what anybody else said about me. It mattered what I said about myself.

When you know your worth and you are confident in who you are, you can thrive in any situation, regardless of what it is. The more you respect yourself the more you will expect and receive respect from others. The more you value your time the more you will protect it. The more you understand the value you bring to any relationship the higher your standards will be.

I became astute at noticing underlying issues of low self-worth in women because I had been there for so long myself. I spoke with women who had no sense of the value of their bodies, so they continually had unprotected sex and became pregnant by men who were known for not taking care of their children. I listened to countless businesswomen who low-balled their prices because they didn't realize the value of what they offered. I heard the cries of women who were stuck in toxic relationships, but debated whether they should leave because they didn't want to be by themselves or feared being labeled as a failure after a divorce. The names and faces were different, but the underlying issue of not knowing their value was the same.

● ● ●

During this time of intense transformation, God shook up my friendships and removed people from my life who wouldn't take this journey with me. Yes, different people are in your life for a reason, a season, or a lifetime, but I had assigned many of my friends to the wrong category. Some of those I thought would be with me for a lifetime were for a season. Some of those I thought would be with me for a season were here with me for a lifetime.

I used to want a few close friends who could fulfill my needs to talk about business, marriage, friendship, shopping, and anything else I desired, but no one person can fulfill all those needs, and no one has to. One of my closest business girlfriends is a single mother. My closest spiritual girlfriend is married and in women's ministry. My friend I talk to most about raising my sons works a nine-to-five job and has no clue what it's like to be a business owner.

The process of going from "I'm not good enough" to "I'm just enough," and finally to "Actually, I'm pretty awesome" took me years and lots of hard work. I didn't just wake up one day, look in the mirror, and watch it magically happen. I had to go through a process of healing, forgiveness, and grieving the life I had lost. Some people think grieving is just for the loss of a loved one's life, but it is also for the loss of a life you once had and will never have again.

The turning point for me came when I stopped listening to what everybody was saying to me about who I was and what

I should do with my life and started tapping into my own intuition and God's voice. It was a lonely place at times, but it was where I needed to be to become the woman God had called me to be.

I started a daily spiritual practice of meditation, affirmations, prayer, praise, and worship. I opened my spirit to hear from God and receive direction. I listened to great spiritual warriors like Priscilla Shirer, who teaches on how fulfilling it is to live a life of submission to God and your family. I filled my phone with gospel tracks, including "I Give Myself Away," by William McDowell, "Never Would Have Made It," by Marvin Sapp, "Break Every Chain," by Tasha Cobbs Leonard, "It's Not Over," by Israel & New Breed, and "I'm Yours," by Casey J, to name a few.

I also learned to be in tune with what was happening around me. I didn't want to keep repeating the same mistakes in my life. I wanted to learn the lesson I was supposed to learn and move on to the next thing.

I love the way Cheryl Richardson, *New York Times* bestselling author of *The Art of Extreme Self Care* (Hay House, 2009) sums it up:

"Life sends us messages
all the time and when we don't hear the message we
get a lesson.
If we don't learn the lesson,
we then get a problem.

And if we don't handle the problem,
we get a full-blown crisis."

Get the message.

I was ready to start learning my lessons and gain valuable insight from the mistakes of others, starting with figuring out how the two shall become one.

Therefore shall a man leave his father and his mother, and shall cleave unto his wife: and they shall be one flesh.

GENESIS 2:24

Chapter 23
The Two Shall Become One

One Friday night, I spent a regular girls' night in with my godsister. I guess I should say a family night in because my house was filled with five busy kids running around and playing. Once a month, my godsister and I got together to catch up and have some good ole girlfriend chatting, and this night, she brought a movie for us to watch. I wasn't prepared for it. This movie brought me to tears and made me realize all kinds of things about my marriage.

I had expected to watch *War Room* and have a great discussion about it. However, watching this movie gave me much more than interesting conversation. It was a major turning point for me in my marriage. *War Room* changed my life and the way I looked at marriage. It showed me the battles we face in marriage are not with our husbands, but they are spiritual battles that must be fought and won in prayer. The movie showed me that arguing, fussing, pouting, and complaining in my marriage was not only wrong, but also useless.

(If you have not seen *War Room*, put this book down and find a way to watch it now. If your mind and heart are open, it will forever change your marriage.)

After watching the movie, I repented, prayed for forgiveness, and started to shift the way I operated in my marriage. I began praying over my husband, my marriage, and myself, asking God to make me into the wife He wanted me to be. I rearranged my priorities so my husband and children all came before my business. I also made sure I was at *the top* of my priority list because if I wasn't taken care of, then I couldn't take care of anybody else.

Honestly, I didn't want to do the work required for me to be in a place of consistent submission. It was a real struggle for me, but I knew I had to do it. I had to learn how to keep my mouth closed and become more sensitive to the needs of my husband. I had to learn how to listen instead of talking. This was particularly challenging for me because, as a certified coach, I ask questions and talk for a living. My husband tells me that for every one word he says, I say 10,000, and he's probably not far off with that estimate. This part of my evolution tested my patience, will, and seriousness about changing.

In essence, I had to die—die to my flesh, die to what I always wanted, and trust God would work through my husband to do what was best for our family. I had to unlearn much of what I thought about marriage and my role as a wife. I had to learn what a healthy marriage looked like and how to hold a common vision for our relationship.

I could no longer think in terms of "I," even when it came to my business. I now had to think in terms of "we." For every major decision I made, I had to consider how it would affect us, not just me. This wasn't instinctive for me and required some major mind shifting.

I also had to learn how to empathetically listen instead of preparing my response or my argument in my mind while my husband was talking. (I know you don't do that. It's just me). I had to truly listen to what he was saying, place myself in his shoes, and listen to hear what he needed. Then—and here's the kicker—when he told me what he needed, I actually had to be willing to do it, rather than thinking he didn't really need what he asked for and I didn't want to do it anyway.

I learned most men don't communicate a lot about their feelings. My husband certainly didn't, so when he did, it was in my best interest to listen. Bishop T. D. Jakes often says, "Give your husband time to process his thoughts." When I felt like something was bothering my husband, but he said nothing was wrong when I asked him about it, I had to just give him time instead of badgering him to talk when I wanted to talk.

If I wanted my husband to communicate with me, I had to give him the opportunity to do it his way. I learned it was important not to interrupt him when he spoke, and even though it wasn't easy for me, I worked on it every day. (One of the books and audio studies that helped me learn how men think was *He-motions*, by T. D. Jakes. I highly recommend it.)

I burned the bonnet, figuratively speaking, dusted off my lingerie drawer, and started putting on something a little more appealing than my lumberjack pants, as my husband calls them. Since men tend to be visual, I switched out my furry house shoes for my stripper stilettos heels (you know the ones you don't wear out in public). I also put down my phone and increased my marriage ministry, a.k.a. making love with my husband.

Most importantly, I prayed for God's direction on how to handle certain situations instead of responding with my gut reaction, which in most cases wasn't the right response. I read scriptures about how the wife is supposed to adjust to her husband. I read them and read them again, and once I realized the words on the page weren't going to change, I dissected the scriptures about mutual submission. I also studied how the husband could be won by the actions of his wife. I had to really grab hold of the idea that he could be won by my actions and not my words. Staying quiet was hard for me sometimes, and it still is.

I was studying intently and learning how to be a godly wife. This was a bit different from what I had done in the past, which was a very good thing. This time, I was embracing my femininity and learning how to enjoy relaxing in the comfort of being a woman and wife and not always having to control everything.

I learned how to tone down my masculinity and tap into my femininity when I was at home. In business, I decided what I wanted, created a strategy, went after it, and almost always got it. I was responsible for making decisions, and I was always in control. That was great in business, but bringing that same energy home often usurped my husband's authority and had us bumping heads.

Learning how to let my husband lead without my help was a hard lesson for me. It meant keeping my mouth closed sometimes, when I wanted to say something, and letting God work in my husband. It meant being supportive of what my husband was doing even when I didn't want to be. We would, of course, talk things out, but ultimately it was his responsibility to lead our household.

As time passed, this became easier for me, but I in no way mastered it. Some days, I did really well, others, not so much. I learned not to beat myself up when I missed the mark. Instead, I assessed what I could have done better in the situation and applied it on the next go-round.

The beauty in all of this was that, as I changed, my husband automatically changed too. I didn't force him to change or ask him to do things differently. As I changed the way in which I responded and reacted, in return, he changed how he responded and reacted to me.

When my husband feels respected and heard and receives cooperation from me, he, in return, loves and embraces me. In most cases, it's a cycle; when a man feels respected, he loves his wife. When a man feels disrespected, he withdraws his love. When a woman feels loved, she respects her husband. When a woman doesn't feel loved, she withdraws her respect or disrespects her husband. The problem is one person has to get off the wrong cycle and start the right one. If you are both waiting on the other to do it first, then you'll remain in the crazy cycle. So whoever is reading this book and gaining the knowledge, unfortunately (or fortunately, depending on your point of view) it's you who will probably be the first one to make the change.

God said to me often, "You are expecting a harvest in your marriage for a seed that you've never sown." In other words, if you've not sown consistent respect in your marriage, then why are you waiting to receive a harvest of consistent love? Drop the mic—enough said. Ouch!

I also learned creating a safe and peaceful environment my husband wanted to come home to was so important. If he felt like he was going to be attacked when he talked to me or like every conversation was going to result in an argument, he preferred to be in his man cave or out playing golf. My role was to create an environment that encouraged intimacy, open communication, carefrontation (not confrontation), and mutual love.

I had more clarity and peace, and my children were experiencing the fruits of my labor. I was no longer waiting on someone else to make me happy; I was creating my own happiness. As a result, our home was filled with more laughter and fun.

Additionally, God prospered my business and opened doors I never could have imagined walking through. I was comfortable in my lane and truly enjoying the benefits of a submitted life. Once priority one, my self-care, and priority two, my husband, were in place, I turned my attention to priority number three, my children.

Mothers hold their children's hands for a moment and their hearts for a lifetime.

_____

AUTHOR UNKNOWN

Chapter 24
The Joy of Motherhood

O nce my marriage was getting back on track—at least for the moment—it was time to turn my focus to my children. The first thing I did was to stop working each day at three in the afternoon, instead of working until five o'clock, so I had fifteen to thirty minutes to decompress, meditate, or relax before I picked up the kids from school. When I went straight from work to picking up my kids, I was often irritable, and my patience quickly wore thin. I yelled more and anxiously waited for their bedtime. Surprisingly, those few minutes of peace made all the difference in the world in the way I interacted with them.

I also stopped burning the candles at both ends, working until two in the morning, and getting right back to work at five thirty. Sleeping for only three or four hours a night wasn't sustainable, and if I kept that habit long enough, it would eventually have a negative impact not just on my family relationships, but also on my health and my productivity. The sacrifice of sleep had short-term benefits, but in the long term, it would have cost me dearly.

I had to define what I wanted the role of mother to look like for me so I wouldn't be overwhelmed with everybody's expectations. I pushed the expectations of my husband, mother, friends, and society out of my head and determined what being a successful mother looked like to me. I also stopped comparing myself to other mothers and the way they parented. I learned how to start playing by my own rules.

In this process, I took a long and hard look at how I was raised. I identified and evaluated the parenting skills my mom and dad had passed down to me. I had to be honest about which worked and which were ineffective. I had to choose which to keep and which to let end with my generation. I also talked to our daughter about what she liked and didn't like about how she was raised. After processing all this information, I started to create a picture of what I wanted my role as a mother to be.

The principal purpose of my role as a mother was to provide a stable, loving, accepting, and engaging home. I wanted to be very present and involved in my children's lives, and open and honest communication was a must. I needed my children to know they could talk to me about anything without fear of punishment or repercussions. I needed them to know that, even if I didn't approve of what they were saying, it was a safe environment for them to be honest.

I realized I had to be very active in their school and extra-curricular activities so I could know their friends and develop great relationships with their teachers. I also needed to challenge them and set high expectations while meeting them where they were and allowing each of them to play to their own strengths. In the process, it was important to be patient and understanding when things didn't work out as planned.

I established my own boundaries, in reference to respect and discipline, and determined what was comfortable for me. I read a ton of books on parenting and even completed a Breakthrough Parent coach certification program, which totally changed the foundation of how I parented. It helped me understand I needed to raise my children to seek internal validation from themselves. They didn't need to look for external validation and approval from me, their father, grandparents, peers, teachers, or other people. It taught me how to discipline with love rather than using psychological or physical punishments to temporarily get my children to do what I wanted them to do. I had to invest the time to help them develop their own internal compass so they would make good decisions for themselves whether I was around or not.

I created structure and routine so my kids would know what was expected of them, and I set boundaries around mommy time to make sure I could regroup and reenergize and be ready to pour into my children again. That could mean a trip to the spa, a lunch date with girlfriends, or thirty minutes alone in my room to reconnect with myself so I could connect with my children.

I removed the word "perfect" from my vocabulary and replaced it with "efficient." I embraced the fact that things aren't always going to happen as I expect. I may think things are going to turn out one way, and the script may get flipped. I learned how to be okay with that and simply go with the flow as much as possible.

● ◉ ●

While I learned a lot, and implemented what I learned as quickly and effectively as I could, this wasn't a journey without hills to climb. Potty training our youngest son was just one of many parenting tasks that challenged me. One summer day, I was so excited because he'd gone several days with no accidents, and I was totally feeling myself, like I was mom of the year. A few hours later, we went to the pool, and my son made it known that he didn't want to keep his swim shorts on. I went from walking around with my chest puffed out, just minutes earlier, to hiding my head between my legs while my son hollered and screamed because he wanted to run naked around the pool. (My youngest has a free spirit; can you tell?) I'm sure the mothers were looking at me and wishing I'd control my child, but I acted like I didn't see them, put his swim trunks on, and continued to swim. I didn't miss a beat.

I couldn't concern myself with how people looked at me or judged my parenting. Parenting was, and would continue to be, a learning experience, and I'd have to take one day at a time to make it through and do the best I possibly could while enjoying my children at each stage of life.

I also stopped comparing my children to other children. Instead, I focused on my own children and their individual needs and gifts. Then I asked God for direction.

I was so stressed out when my children were younger and didn't hit some of the milestones the doctors said they should right on time or couldn't perform certain tasks at the level of other kids in their class. I wondered if I was doing something wrong. Was I not a good mother? Why was my child not meeting the milestones? I looked for comfort from doctors and teachers, but this was something I had to get comfortable with for myself. I learned to stop comparing their development and growth to their peers and simply focused on what they needed at that time so I could give it to them.

These changes required me to relinquish control. I had tried to micromanage everything from what my kids ate and wore to bedtime, reading time, and how homework was done. At one point, I was trying to get my younger son in bed by eight thirty at night. So for weeks, probably months, we battled and battled. I'd put him in the bed, and he'd get up and just talk and sing until about ten thirty or eleven o'clock every night, and I took it personally. I just knew my son had it out for me and didn't want me to sleep. I'm a morning person, so I prefer to go to bed before ten at night, and I needed my son to cooperate to make this happen. Of course, he had other plans.

After getting completely frustrated by his behavior, I had to do something different. I looked at his sleep patterns and realized on the days he took a nap at school, he stayed up late at night, and on the days he didn't take a nap, he fell asleep earlier. He was a night person, not an early riser, and I had to adjust the way I put him to bed at night. Once I shifted from trying to control and force him and started observing his patterns and creating a schedule based on his needs, life got much easier for both of us.

I was brought up to do what my parents said to do. Unfortunately, that didn't work with my son and trying to make him so obedient only frustrated us both. As I talked with other parents, I noticed many of them were experiencing similar issues with their children and were at the end of their ropes trying to figure out a solution. Once we all took a step back, assessed the situation, and responded to our child's needs instead of what the Internet and old-school parenting books taught us, we noticed positive shifts in our children's lives.

As I delved deeper into research on parenting, I found helpful resources. One great book on parenting a highly motivated and active child was *Authentic Parenting Power*, by Sandi Schwartz. It helped me redefine my role as a mother and understand how my two boys were wired. I also ran across a phenomenal book called *Promises Kept: Raising Black Boys to Succeed in School and in Life*, by Joe Brewster, MD, and Michèle Stephenson. Enlightening and insightful, this book described the different learning styles of boys, the best ways to educate and motivate them, and how positive parenting affects our boys.

I also started to use some of my coaching techniques with my kids. I let them have a voice and vision for their own lives.

Instead of always telling them what they were going to do, I gave options (of course, I would have been fine with either of the options I gave them), and this allowed them to develop their independence and decision-making skills and learn to deal with the natural consequences of their choices.

My older son developed critical thinking and decision-making skills by choosing how he wanted to dress and what extracurricular activities he wanted to participate in. When it came to homework, if he wanted to do it standing up or running around, that was fine with me. I no longer fought with him to get him to sit down in a chair after he had been at school, sitting at a desk, for more than seven hours. He wanted some freedom, flexibility, and movement, a small price to pay for getting homework completed without arguments or a bad attitude.

I had two very active young boys, and the way they learned was different from the way most schools taught. They were both kinesthetic and visual learners and learned best with hands-on application. I researched for hours, weeks—it felt like years—to find the right school for my older son, one with small class sizes and project-based learning, because the traditional school setting with large class sizes and filling in worksheets all day wasn't a good fit for him.

I had to be proactive in finding the right school. He was smart and caught on quickly, but he needed to be highly engaged. I visited several schools, where I spoke with teachers and principals, until I found the right fit. After an exhausting search, I finally enrolled my older son in a school where he could learn in the ways that worked best for him and truly thrive.

● ◦ ●

I went through a similar process with my younger son, and this time around challenged me even more. His teachers found he sometimes couldn't care less about circle time or socializing with his peers. He was just as happy playing in his own world or doing educational games on a tablet. It was frustrating to walk in the classroom and find every student following the rules and on task except my child. It took some blood, sweat, and a whole lot of tears to find the right teacher for him and to make sure he received the love and compassion he needed.

My friends' kids seemed to reach all the milestones—talking, potty training, writing, sharing, socializing—right on time, but my younger son hadn't read the parenting books. He arrived at each milestone on his own schedule and simply learned differently from other kids, even his older brother. In trying to understand his needs and make the best decisions for him, I felt so alone. I had my husband to talk to, of course, but how would my friends understand what I was going through when they had never experienced it? It seemed like their kids sat down when their parents said sit and always acted right during school plays or at restaurants. I wondered if there was any other mother in the world who could relate to what I was going through. If so, could she please stand up?

Fortunately, after many exhausting conversations with mothers of my sons' classmates, talking with women in the grocery store whose sons had just thrown a tantrum, and reading posts on mommy blogs, I realized I wasn't alone. I found support with moms who were going through the same things I was. Your journey is always easier when you have a fellow mom on the road with you.

● ● ●

After enrolling both boys in schools where their educational needs could be met, I started cooking more or at least planning my meals so I could cook one or two days a week and make enough for leftovers. This reduced the stress of figuring out what was for dinner with two hungry children walking in the door after school demanding, "Mommy, what are we going to eat?" Before, I would have no clue until I looked in the refrigerator to see what I could quickly throw together. I also identified healthy restaurant choices for those occasions when I needed to pick up a quick meal.

Fresh, nutritious meals laid the foundation for me to focus on living a healthier lifestyle and support my husband and kids in doing the same. I incorporated meditation into our morning and evening routines. As a family, we started taking multivitamins, probiotics, and DHA/omega-3, and we made it a point to drink more water. These small changes didn't require a lot of time or effort, but they made a big difference to our overall health, and I felt good about giving our kids the chance to develop good habits early in life.

I intentionally became more emotionally, mentally, and physically present for my family. Instead of texting during homework or story time, I focused my complete attention on my children. I spent at least twenty minutes with each of my sons before bed, including playtime and storytime, which allowed us to bond over fun activities. I went on more field trips, volunteered more at school, and made the conscious decision to enjoy my kids as much as possible.

Cutting back on activities was critical to this transition to our new identity as a more present and mindful family. As parents, we want the best for our children, and this desire to see them have more and be more can overwhelm us and them. It's so easy to get caught up in pushing them to achieve. We want them to be honor roll students, play sports, take karate, play an instrument in the band, and do any and everything that might give them a greater chance of success later in life.

This often leads to burn-out for us, from having to chauffeur our kids everywhere, and pure exhaustion for them, from doing so much and rarely having downtime to just be kids. Just as adults need time to grow bored and figure out what to do with their time, daydream and imagine, pursue their interests with no goal in mind, and learn to be alone with themselves, so do kids. These essential skills are impossible for kids to develop when they're constantly occupied with schoolwork and activities.

● ● ●

Every mother brings her own set of strengths and gifts to her role as a parent, and I realized I wasn't yet making the most of mine. I'd always been focused and strategic in business plan-ning, but I'd never done that kind of planning with my children. That was about to change. I identified the top three things I wanted to work on with each of my children and focused on doing just those three things. These ideas became the basis for our family plan, a list of goals for my children and our plan to accomplish those goals.

My focus for my older son was ensuring he learned more responsibility by consistently doing his chores, increased his critical thinking for decision-making, and improved his read-ing comprehension. With my younger son, we focused on potty training, speaking more in conversations, and learning to write. Writing these goals down in our family plan made it clear where we should devote our time and attention and allowed me to let go of other goals I might have had for the boys, but which were less important at the time.

When I was pregnant with each of my children, I prayed for strong leaders. However, I meant they should be that way when they were grown and out of my house, not during the toddler and adolescent years. Be careful what you pray for. My sons possess all the strong traits of leaders. They're inde-pendent thinkers and confident, innovative risk-takers. They know exactly what they want, how they want it, and when they want it. The "because I said so" style of parenting was never going to work for them.

My oldest son's first response to "Because I said so" was "*Why* do you say so?" He wasn't being disrespectful, but he's very analytical and things need to make sense to him. Once I explained the why behind my request to him, he immediately did what I asked. However, at six in the morning, I didn't often feel like explaining.

Couple this with the will of my younger son, who couldn't be bribed or forced to potty train because he marched to the beat of his own music. Rewards, treats, and the sticker chart did nothing for him. I thought I could coach or motivate anybody to do anything, but apparently my powers have no effect on my son. The SuperMommy cape I'd dreamed of wearing came off fast.

Since I didn't have all the answers, I read books and listened to audio trainings on parenting and on raising a strong-willed child. I had to learn patience. I had to learn not to compare my child to anybody else, not even his sibling. I had to learn to really study each child as an individual because everything you read in books or talk about with other parents will not apply to your child. I had to learn to forgive myself on the days when I messed up.

Motherhood was by far the most rewarding job for me, but also the hardest. I had to understand I was responsible for giving my kids my best and raising them to the best of my ability, but I had to keep in mind that they had their own will and made their own decisions. I could raise them to have character, integrity, compassion, and a strong work ethic, but in the end, each of my sons would choose his own path.

Some days, I felt like I slam-dunked as a mother, and I celebrated my success. Other days, I felt like I couldn't get a shot in to save my life and might need some time on the bench.

Some days, I did everything on our list, and other days, we were good just to get out of the house and get to school on time. In the end, I prayed for them every day, and I worked on being the best woman I could be because they learned more by my actions than my words.

As soon as I could, I surrounded myself with other mothers on similar journeys, so I didn't feel so alone in this thing called motherhood. As mothers, we can be so hard on ourselves, wondering if we're giving our children everything they need to thrive in life. I came to realize our children are rarely concerned with the material possessions we can provide. They're most interested in our time, creating fun experiences, developing traditions they can past down to their families, and being loved unconditionally. In that spirit, I encourage every mother to give herself a break when she feels like she's falling short.

In addition to praying for my children, I developed a habit of speaking daily affirmations over them, and they repeated these "I am" statements.

I am smart.
I am wise.
I am healthy.
I am wealthy.
I am prosperous.
I am loved.
I am fearless.
I am favored.

I am a conqueror.
I am a good decision-maker.
I am a leader.
I am at peace.
I am calm.

Every word that came after "I am" was what would man-ifest in my child's life. And because I believed every word that came after "I am" would manifest in my child's life, I also made sure not to speak words of death or negativity over my children.

You're stupid.
You never listen.
You can't do anything right.
You're a failure.
You get on my nerves.
You make me sick.
You're just like your father (and not saying it in a good way)!

Those kinds of statements, even when said in anger and without intention, are detrimental to a healthy self-esteem and sense of self-worth. These statements are also absolute, describing the child as a person, rather than addressing his behavior. All parents experience frustrations with our kids, but I realized we must be careful about how we handle them. We must be intentional, positive, and uplifting with the words we speak over our children.

Our children internalize what we say about them, and those words can become a self-fulfilling prophecy in their lives. If I call my children liars, they will lie. If I tell them they're stupid, they will believe me and behave accordingly. I made the conscious decision every day to tell them how smart, loving, and honest they are. It created a level of expectation in our family and held them accountable for setting high expectations for themselves.

While my kids sometimes messed up, so did I. I had to learn how to apologize to them and mean it. When I made mistakes, got easily frustrated, forgot something, or lost my temper, I had to own it and ask for forgiveness. This simple act of apologizing gave my children an opportunity to practice forgiveness and compassion. It also taught them they didn't have to be right about everything and it was okay to admit when they were wrong and apologize too. Rather than make me appear weak, apologizing made me stronger in their eyes and my own because I accepted responsibility for my actions, a character trait I wanted to instill in them.

If I had an off day and yelled at my children, I owned it. "Mommy is really tired, and I'm getting irritated and upset because you're not listening to me. I apologize for yelling because I shouldn't do that. Now, I need you to do what I asked." Most times, my sons heard the sincerity or frustration (whichever you prefer) in my voice and got in line without further discussion. Since I didn't want a household where yelling was the norm, I proactively utilized other approaches to keep peace in my home and my children's emotional wellbeing intact.

During our nighttime routine, regardless of what happened during the day, my sons ended their night with gratitude, prayer, at least one compliment from me about a positive thing they did, one thing they were proud of themselves for, and a good-night kiss and hug. This routine went a long way in helping them have a good night's sleep.

Regardless of how hectic our mornings were, before they got out of the car, I told them how special and smart they were and how much I loved them. I wished them a wonderful day, and we spoke affirmations over their life. This way, my sons walked into school with a positive mindset and ready to learn.

My husband also created his own routine for ensuring a positive day for our children. During the drive to school, he talked with our sons about their friends, what they enjoyed most at school, or anything else that positively engaged them. This facilitated / allowed open communication between them and encouraged our sons to feel comfortable talking with us about their lives outside of our home.

Early on, when I asked my kids how their day at school went, they'd give me one-word answers, like "Fine," which told me nothing about their day. Clearly, I had to change the questions I asked. I started to engage my children in conversation with specific, open-ended questions. I did this without making them feel like I was prying into their business because I was answering the same questions about my day for them. We had conversation instead of interrogation.

My husband and I encouraged open discussion at the dinner table with several questions:

What made you happy and/or sad today?
What was one fun thing you did?
What was one thing you learned?
What one thing made you proud of yourself?

I came to see the best gift and advantage I could give my children was the chance to become whole, live free from fear, guilt, and shame, and be clear about what they really want in life. I had to learn how to do these things myself so I could pass them on to my children. Along with my husband, I had to provide our children with a firm foundation of self-love, authenticity, confidence, and boldness to step into their purpose.

When everyone else says you can't, determination says, 'Yes, you can.'

ROBERT M. HENSEL

Chapter 25
Diagnosis Doesn't Mean Defeat

D-Day was finally here. No, it wasn't the day of final reckoning in the latest superhero movie release. It was the day my youngest son received a diagnosis on the autism spectrum. My husband and I sat up straight in our chairs as the psychologist went through a forty-page report. She was telling us all the findings that led her to the diagnosis of autism, but as she spoke, my mind seemed to leave my body. I heard her words, but I didn't fully comprehend them.

Our son was four years old, and doctors had been telling us for years that he wasn't reaching his milestones at the appropriate times. I always knew he was a little different. I thought he had developmental delays, and of course, I did what any momma bear would do. I put aside any feelings that came up for me and leaped straight into action. I went into pure research and fix-it mode. I consumed every bit of information I could put my hands on, books, videos, and trainings. I was going to tackle this head-on. It would be my son and me against the world; he would defy all the odds. Receiving the diagnosis gave me a sharper focus for all that research and study.

The first plan of action was assembling his team, which consisted of a BCBA (Board Certified Behavior Analyst) therapist, an ABA (Applied Behavior Analyst) therapist, a speech therapist, and an occupational therapist. I became obsessed with making sure he had what he needed. Therapy appointments and research consumed my life.

Yes, my son received a diagnosis from the doctor and was told at the time that he was low functioning and had limits on his life. However, I never spoke any of that over him. I chose to speak life over him and prophesy about who he would become and all the things he would accomplish. From the beginning, I surrounded him with a team of people who saw the genius in him.

During this time, I felt incredibly isolated because, outside of his therapists and immediate family, I didn't share my son's diagnosis with anyone. I often felt like he had a red mark next to his name because he stood out from other children his age. He didn't want to sit down during circle time. He struggled with focusing for long periods of schoolwork. He was very active, non-verbal, and not potty trained until the middle of kindergarten. He didn't handle the word "no" well and would have huge tantrums that lasted for what seemed like hours because his body was on sensory overload.

The journey of raising a child with special abilities is life changing. It can either change you for the better or for the worse. It can tear your family apart, or it can bring your family together. It can totally control your life, or you can learn how to lean into this new path. It can cultivate your faith or totally consume you with fear.

My son has been the biggest blessing to me because he has taught me unconditional love, patience, the danger of labels, and the power of affirmations, prayer, and positive thinking. Framing his difference as special abilities and learning differently, instead of special needs, was a game changer for me. It allowed me to really focus on all the amazing qualities and gifts he has and to help him cultivate them. He continues to teach me way more than I could ever teach him, and God continues to amaze me as I look into his eyes every day. My son has helped me understand the true meaning of parenting each child based on their unique and individual needs.

Whether your child has a diagnosis or not, allow God to have His hand in there. Your child's path may not look like what you think it should look like, and you have to be okay what that. In my case, my mom thought me going to prison was the worst thing that could happen to me, but it was where my purpose was actually born.

Your life is not over if your child receives a diagnosis—whether it's dyslexia, ADD, ADHD, autism, cerebral palsy, Down syndrome, or another physical or intellectual difference. Yes, your child may be different from other children, but you and God can be a strong committee of two and figure out what your child needs to live an abundant life. Pray over your children and allow God to lead their path. It will all work out for their good regardless of what it looks like today.

● ◦ ●

Raising teenagers, it turns out, is just as challenging as everyone says it is. When I was pregnant with both of my sons, I asked God for strong-willed kids. He granted that request. However, I wasn't clear in asking for that to happen once they moved out of the house, not starting at birth. My older son truly holds a mirror up to me, daily. He's smart, intuitive, outspoken, and driven. He knows what he wants, and he's not afraid to ask for it. He reminds me that he's watching everything I do. "Do as I say, not as I do" absolutely does not work with him.

My oldest son has truly helped me up-level who I am and how I parent. One of those learning moments occurred when he was ready to enter high school and we discussed the possibility of him applying for a prestigious magnet program. I secretly wanted him to apply, and although I tried to remain neutral in our conversation, I pointed out all the pros of applying to the program. Mid-stream in the conversation, my son said, "Mom, it sounds like you're attempting to influence my decision. You raised me to be an independent thinker and to make decisions on my own."

Wait, what? I've lost my influence on your decisions? What a conflicting moment. I felt proud of the independence my son displayed. At the same time, I had to accept that he had one foot outside of our house and was one step closer to living his own life.

From his out-of-control hair to his skinny jeans and fitted clothes and his decision to not discuss any potential girlfriend until he's ready, my son has, in no uncertain terms, challenged my comfort level with so many things. He forced me to consciously focus on the type of mother I want to be to him. So many of us say, "I'm not going to be like my mom," and we wake up one day and find we are exactly that. However, I realized I don't want to make decisions for my kids. I want to teach them how to make decisions. I don't want to be controlling. I want to teach my kids how to take full control of their lives by trusting their intuition and going after their dreams. I learned to replace a lot of limiting beliefs about parenting that no longer served me and to listen to my children about what's important to them in our relationship. I learned how to teach them to validate and express their own emotions and feelings whether I agree with them or not.

Especially during the teen years, raising an independent and self-aware child is not for the faint of heart. It challenges you at the core of who you are and will stretch you to the point of no return. One day, when I got angry, my older son looked at me and said, "Mom, take three deep breaths, calm down, and remember it's going to be okay." That moment of compassion and wisdom was a return on the investment I'd made in him. You never know what your child is absorbing from the seeds you're sowing. Keep planting and watering, and God will truly give your child the increase.

● ○ ●

How dare I desire another baby after I turned forty? The nerve of me still wanting a baby after forty-five! The medical community calls any pregnancy after thirty-five a geriatric pregnancy. The message is that you've waited too late and your hopes of having a family are slim to none.

We live with such a double standard when it comes to this subject. Men receive a very different message: Just marry a younger woman and have kids at any age you want. Men can wait until their seventies to have kids, and few people will call them selfish.

I had my first child at thirty-three and my second child at thirty-seven. However, I still had room in my heart for just one more special bundle of joy, a little girl. I've wanted a daughter since my childhood days of playing with dolls. I was thrilled when God gave me my bonus daughter, when she was fourteen, through my marriage to Anthony, and I loved having her in my life. She was such a joy for me, and at the same time, I wanted a little girl I could raise from her earliest days of be-ribboned headbands, holiday dresses, and mother-daughter dates. No amount of pouring into our oldest child or mentoring young women and girls ever removed that desire.

When I was pregnant with my younger son, I thought he was a girl. Thank God He knew what I needed. My son is the apple of my eye, my miracle baby, my blessing. I wouldn't change a thing about who he is. At the same time, over the decade that followed, the desire to have a daughter never left me. I felt like I was meant to be the mother of another daughter because I had so much to share with her. I wanted the kind of close mother-daughter relationship I didn't have with my mom.

I prayed if it wasn't God's will for me to have a daughter, that He take the desire from me. The desire remained, but I reached a level of acceptance. It has taken me more than ten years to come to a place of recognizing my life is completely full whether I add a daughter to my family or not.

In so many cases, people attempt to make women feel bad or doubt themselves for wanting to have kids later in life. I looked for years for a safe space with other women of color who wanted kids after forty. I never found it. All I found were lists of the many risks that come with a later-in-life pregnancy. I was told I had waited too late, and it probably would never happen for me.

Most of my friends in my inner circle couldn't wait until their kids graduated from high school, so I didn't feel there was anyone around me who could understand my desire for a child in my mid-forties. If you feel the same way, I hear you, I see you, I am you. Acknowledge and honor that longing, and know you're okay.

Maybe you were focused on climbing the corporate ladder or building a business in your twenties and thirties. Maybe you didn't have the right partner yet. Or maybe life simply didn't work out as planned. Whatever the reason, if you have a desire to have kids later in life, don't beat yourself up for waiting. Honor your desire in whatever ways you can.

You may still be blessed with a child, but if it never happens, you can still feel your feelings and honor them. I silenced my voice for a long time, and I'm no longer doing that. Honor your voice. Pursue the path God is leading you to and leading you on. You are honored and valued, your desire is honored and valued, and your voice is heard.

A great marriage is not when the "perfect couple" comes together. It is when an imperfect couple learns to enjoy their differences.

DAVE MEURER

Chapter 26
Who God Has Put Together, Let Not the Ego Separate

W ho said marriage will always go the way you want it to? Apparently, I did, but that was such misguided thinking. Late one evening during the pandemic, my husband and I were having a discussion. I have no idea how the conversation escalated, but it ended when my husband told me he wanted a divorce. This wasn't an ultimatum, as he'd given me in the past. He uttered those words in the heat of our disagreement—as I imagine happens in many marital spats— but that one sentence would have an unintended impact on our relationship.

Those words, "I want a divorce," didn't register with me until days later. Already at a crossroads in my life, I realized I had to make some hard decisions. I'd been in therapy for years, and I was finally learning how to validate myself, understand my worth and value, and set boundaries. I knew what I wanted, and I wasn't settling in any area of my life anymore.

Let me paint the picture for you. I'm not a drinker, but imagine a group of friends who hang out together, drink, and have a good time. Then one day, one person gets sober, cold turkey. Now, she's looking at everybody else who's still drinking and judging them for their choice to consume alcohol and how they behave when they do. Or consider the newly saved Christian. She's been going to church for two days and now sees everybody else as a sinner. Sad to say, but that was me. I'd been on my healing journey for a while and had grown exhausted of not getting what I wanted in my marriage. I wanted my husband to change on my schedule and by my agenda, but he wasn't. So I wanted out.

The decisions Anthony and I made over the next four months changed my marriage and my life forever. Reflecting on my husband's words and seeing them as a way out, I had the bright idea of filing for divorce. Everything that had been bubbling up in our marriage for more than a decade came to the surface. At this point, I was all in my masculine alpha energy, bossed up, independent, and singing Beyoncé's "Survivor" as I went through this process. Nobody was going to hold me down. I deserved better.

Because of the pandemic, we still lived in our home together as we went through the divorce proceedings. I stayed on the upper level, and my husband took the lower level. During this time, I bounced around the house like everything was normal. I was all in my ego and buying into the façade and lies social media had sold me. *Be a boss babe. Grow your business at all costs. Kick your spouse to the curb if they don't support you. Sleep when you die!* I was listening to the "experts" and "gurus" on social media, but I was all out of order and walking outside of the will of God.

One day, my car started giving me trouble, and since my husband always handled any car problems, I called him. As Anthony and I talked, God clearly spoke to my spirit. "I never told you to file for divorce," God said.

My first thought was: *Satan, I bind you. Get behind me!* I had already played everything out in my imagination. I'd already redecorated the house in my mind. I knew how my lifestyle would change as soon as I had my freedom. I'd even planned what my new dream marriage would look like. The only problem: I was walking in pure pride and selfishness.

After that conversation, God started to reveal me to me in a new way. He reminded me of what he had told me often. I was expecting a harvest from my marriage for a seed I'd never sown. God showed me how I'd sown and watered seeds for my business, for my kids, and for my dreams, but not for my husband or our marriage.

Next, God hit me with a series of questions. *How have you consistently created a safe space for your husband and for your marriage to grow (not just for a month or two or when you felt like it, but always)?* Well, God stumped me on that one because I hadn't done it consistently. *When have you gone beyond what was convenient for you to show your husband love and respect in a way that didn't involve the children?* Two for two, I had nothing.

As God continued to hold a mirror up to me and help me

understand how I was showing up in my marriage, I fell to my closet floor and cried uncontrollably for three hours. I tried to cry in silence so my kids wouldn't hear me, but I was a mess as God showed me the raw, unfiltered truth about me. Finally, He told me as much as I'd wanted my husband to be different, I was the one who needed to change. He told me to stop focusing on what my husband was supposed to be doing and start sowing the seeds of love I wanted to receive.

Initially, I completely rejected the idea. I felt like I'd been working on the marriage by myself, and my husband had taken me for granted. I went on and on and on, pleading my case about how I didn't have anything left to give my husband. Over the next few days, I prayed, listened to God, worshipped, and finally accepted that all my blessings and abundance were wrapped up in my obedience to God. I could continue to move forward with the divorce proceedings, or I could heed the voice of God, call off the divorce, and focus on becoming the best wife I could be without the expectation of reciprocity. God was calling me to step out in faith and trust Him with both my husband and marriage.

●　●　●

Let me tell you that the process of dying to your will and surrendering to God's bigger purpose for your life can be painful. God was truly doing a rebirth process in me. I was evolving into the next best version of myself. He was making me into something I'd never been. I'm a go-getter, a leader, a let's-make-it-happen, fire-sign Aries. I operate at one speed: faster. But God was calling me to do less and receive more, a foreign concept to me.

I'd always moved a lot in my masculine energy of leadership, action, logic, and focus. Now, God was calling me to operate more in my feminine energy of receiving, responding, intuitive guidance, patience, compassion, empathy, creativity, and intuition. He was showing me how my husband and I often butted heads because I wasn't the yin (feminine) to my husband's yang (masculine). I was always over in his lane, telling him what to do because I thought I was smarter or my ideas were better, even though he'd been in control of his life for quite a while.

I gave God an opportunity to show up on my behalf when I was quiet, and I know in the depths of my soul that God is a restorer, a reconciler, and a healer. God completely shifted my thinking from the belief that something was wrong with my marriage to recognizing my husband and I are both imperfect but perfect for each other. It's not Anthony's job to fix me, and it's not my job to fix him. We can accept each other as we are, ask for what we need and want, and learn how to compromise.

Too often we stand in the way of what God wants to do in our marriage, but if we surrender and humble ourselves, God can use us to develop the marriage we want. Pride and the CEO mentality can cost us the biggest blessing, a loving and fulfilling marriage. If your marriage is struggling, focus on healing yourself and allow God to work in your husband without expecting perfection from him. Where you are now is not where you will always be. As I continue to evolve and reflect, I've learned to take the lessons from what happened in the past, forgive, and continue to move forward. You can too.

I understand now that I have to connect with myself first and know who I am at my core and what I value. Then and only then can I understand what makes me happy, which is totally my responsibility, not my husband's. Only once I'm happy with myself, can I connect with my husband from a place of already being full. It's been a journey and has taken me a long time to get comfortable in my own skin, but it has been worth the effort.

Now that I've gotten a little more relaxed in my feminine energy, I see that when I release control, I'm mindful and present, and I focus on what I should be doing as a wife, many of the things I've been asking for in my marriage appear. Just a few days ago, we came back from vacation in Destin, Florida, where my husband, our sons, and I played on the beach, ate amazing food, and loved life. This wouldn't have happened before because I never left space for it, but I didn't plan one thing for this vacation. My husband booked it all, and I allowed everything to flow and happen without a word of input from me. Every day, I strive to stay in a place of gratitude and surrendering to God so I can continue to attract abundance into my marriage and life. It's an amazing place to be.

Your purpose in life is to find your purpose and give your whole heart and soul to it.

_____

UNKNOWN

Chapter 27
Stepping into Purpose

Years ago, I heard Joyce Meyer make a statement I found very insightful. Instead of praying for God to enlarge your territory and bless your business, she said, you should go take dominion over those dishes in the sink and the dirty laundry. I found her statement so hilarious and so true. In essence, she was saying, before you go and build this global enterprise, make sure your home is taken care of, starting with the basics.

This was exactly what God had me doing as I shifted my priorities. He was telling me to place first things first. He reminded me I needed to get my own house in order before I went to help somebody else get her house in order. I had to mind my own business first.

God was shifting every area of my life, including my business. For years, I'd consulted with corporations and coached business owners to build successful businesses. Leadership development, Diversity, Equity, and Inclusion (DEI); organizational development; and change management were my main areas of focus. I enjoyed doing it, and I was good at it, but I knew it wasn't my heart's truest desire.

I didn't have a burning desire to wake up in the morning and change people's lives with the information I was sharing every day. In fact, I reached a point where I dreaded my work. I wasn't excited about posting on social media, seeing clients, training, or speaking. The flame of my professional desire had slowly died down to a flicker.

At first, I thought I was experiencing burnout. After all, I'd been in business for over twenty years. But as I investigated further, I saw my problem wasn't burnout. I was out of purpose. God had been dealing with me for more than eight years and directing me to teach women how to succeed in their marriage, family, and business, but over and over, I had said no.

I had so many reasons for my refusals. Number one, I was working out my own issues in my marriage and family, so I didn't believe I was ready to teach others how to be successful in those areas yet. Number two, I didn't consider myself an expert, so I couldn't imagine why anyone would listen to me. Number three, I didn't know how I would make money doing that kind of work. Number four, I didn't want to put my personal life on display and be vulnerable and transparent because people would judge me. Number five, the work He wanted me to do was outside of my comfort zone, and I wanted to stay safe, doing what I knew and already did well.

For years upon years, I'd continued to do what I thought was natural and comfortable for me. I continued to coach, speak, and train on business and leadership, until I completely lost the desire for it and took some time off. During my sabbatical, I didn't miss being away from social media. I didn't miss leaders. I didn't care if I was no longer relevant or sought after. Well-meaning folks warned me, "You need to stay in the public eye so people will remember you." But by that point, I didn't care if people forgot my name.

I was fine being a semi-stay-at-home mom, although I still consulted and worked with existing clients. During this time, I found joy in the simple things in life. I wasn't stressed about how many new clients I could get, how much revenue I made for the month, how many likes I got, or how many invitations I received to speak. God was shifting my mindset, causing me to transform my decision-making from personally driven to led by Him. Given the choice, I decided I wanted to walk in purpose and surrender to what God had been asking me to do for years.

During this time, I noticed every business client I had within a period of sixty days came to me with personal issues he or she needed help solving and which were affecting their business productivity. Over the course of many years, the same trend would repeat with woman after woman, man after man. Whether the client had a million-dollar family medical practice, ran a government division with over one thousand employees, or was transitioning from a corporate job to a new business, every issue I coached or consulted on during this period had an underlying factor related to a mindset, traumatic, marital, or familial issue. God was giving me a glimpse of what was to come.

As an adult woman and business owner, I never wanted to be considered a life coach. That role seemed so fluffy and airy to me. It conjured images from movies and TV shows of women and men who spoke in platitudes and asked more questions than they gave answers. I wanted to be known for creating strategies and step-by-step systems for achieving business goals. I resisted dealing with the root causes of most of our issues, our mindset and self-defeating thoughts caused by our life experiences, because they felt like soft areas that were secondary to the work I did. As I let God lead me, I came to see just as we need a business plan we also need a life success plan for our self-care, marriage, and family. There is nothing fluffy or airy about being intentional about the life you want to design for yourself.

Finally, I gave in to what God had been asking me to do and had gifted me to do since I was a young girl. My entire business and brand shifted to The CEO Life. My goal became to help women live a life of abundance in every area: mind, body, spirit, relationships, finances, and business.

I said yes afraid. I said yes not knowing which direction the business was going in or how I would make money. I said yes not knowing if people were going to embrace me. I said yes even though I was working through my own issues. I just said yes and never looked back. I stopped worrying about the how and focused on the what, and as I needed to know the exact steps, instructions appeared.

The minute I said yes, people started coming out of the woodwork, needing my services. New consulting and coaching clients showed up in abundance, and I didn't have to go out and search for them. God showed me when you submit your life to Him, surrender your will, and let Him lead your life, He will always take care of you.

Business is different for me now, and it's filled with new purpose and passion. My work isn't about money. It's about changing lives. It's about shifting the mindset of just one woman so she can shift the trajectory of her whole family. It's about helping women realize the importance of being a whole woman, including being a wife and mother if those are her roles, and not just a business owner or corporate leader. It's about helping women let go of shame, fear, and guilt and forgive themselves. It's coaching women to stop sabotaging their success and stop holding themselves hostage. It's about guiding women to create a vision for their life and supporting them as they make that vision a reality.

Stepping into purpose requires no more excuses, no more lying to yourself, and no more blaming others. It demands that you take full responsibility for where you are, regardless of what was done to you, so you can design the life you desire. It obligates you to grieve the life and relationships you no longer have, forgive those people who have hurt you, and release them from your life. Relationships are for a lifetime, a season, or a reason. Bless those who are not a part of your future, and lovingly send them on their way so you can live fully in your purpose.

My new journey required me to get comfortable telling my story, however uncomfortable, raw, or hurtful it may be. I had

227

to accept that what I went through and the story of how God delivered me was exactly what my sister needed to hear to get through her storms and trials, and I had the power to give her that gift.

The very first step I took to live a life of abundance was to take time out to really understand what my greatest priorities were and then shift my life around to reflect them. You too can take that step when you know you're more than okay just the way you are and God loves you unconditionally. The only way to live your true purpose is to be authentically you, just as God created you to be.

● ● ●

Personal development is professional development (and vice versa), and my personal evolution included my natural hair journey. This process was a healing journey for me. For most of my adult life, I'd operated in corporate spaces where I primarily interacted with white men. For years, I didn't wear braids because I feared those men, and other people I worked with, would judge me as unprofessional. I worried they wouldn't take me seriously if I showed up with braids instead of the straightened hair I, like most Black women my age, had learned to see as acceptable for work.

During the COVID-19 pandemic, I decided to show up in all spaces with my natural hair, and that included wearing braids when the mood struck me. Anyone who couldn't accept all of me would get none of me. While our country was experiencing major protests from the Black Lives Matter movement, this wasn't a "Black power" statement for me. I had no desire to prove anything to anyone. My decision to wear my natural hair was another step towards total acceptance of myself. My hairstyle didn't impact my professionalism or my skills, and if the people I worked with couldn't see that, it would be their loss, not mine.

My clients certainly noticed my change of hairstyle, and many had no problem expressing their opinion about it. One after another, they told me they loved it. It turned out that, in many cases, I'd been projecting my fears and internalized biases on other people. If anyone had a problem with my hair, they kept it to themselves, and it never impacted my business in a negative way. Even if someone had spoken up to complain about my braids, I would have been okay. I was becoming more of the me I was created to be every day. Each day I grew more comfortable being authentically me.

●　○　●

I was talking with the massage therapist during a massage session when she said to me, "You're the CEO Healer. You help heal the mindset, which determines every other thing in that person's life." She was right, and that vision of myself as a healer was a part of my rebirth. I'd been so busy chasing the idea that I could help people build and grow a successful business that I'd forgotten about the whole person in that CEO seat. God had told me from the beginning that my business acumen and experience were just there to build my credibility and encourage women to listen to me and trust me. My purpose was never about business. It was always about healing the mindset and healing the heart.

My ministry is disguised in business. Every day I wake up and talk to these women, I am doing ministry masquerading as business. This is me being obedient so God can speak through me. I have finally embraced that I am a CEO Healer. Part of my gifting is to help heal CEOs so they can be the wife, mom, and business owner they were meant to be. I help them leave a generational legacy for their family, co-create with God in their feminine nature, and walk in their purpose without chasing money. I coach them to achieve health and prosperity by allowing God to heal them and develop them into the next best version of themselves. This is 360-degree abundance.

I'm embracing my role as a mindset surgeon, identifying and helping remove limiting beliefs and subconscious thoughts holding women back. I guide women to identify the negative stories they have about themselves and then rewrite those stories. When they go through this process, how they show up as a woman, wife, and CEO changes. This is the next level for me. Everything I did in my work with corporate America set the stage for the work I'm doing now. This is where God is sending me, and this book is a catapult for it all.

Create a life that feels good on the inside, not one that just looks good on the outside.

AUTHOR UNKNOWN

Chapter 28
Making Sense of It All

On a summer morning filled with Georgia sunshine, promising a hot afternoon, I prepared to facilitate a strategy session for one of my corporate clients. A catered breakfast had been delivered and laid out for attendees. I had my training presentation and workbooks ready to go. From head to toe, I was sharp in my fitted green dress with black trimming and matching shoes. Everything, it appeared, was as it should be. It was going to be a good day.

Eight leaders (five white men, one white woman, and two Black women) gathered around the glass conference table. From the outset, they participated and engaged with the material, but there was one major problem. They were, in essence, having the same conversation we'd had the previous month—and the month before that. Worse, they were discussing the same things brought to the table almost eight months earlier.

Nothing had changed. The company hadn't implemented any of the strategies we'd come up with, and they had no results to measure. This was how most of the meetings had gone, one after the other, month after month, but it had never bothered me. The client always paid on time, and I was fine with our routine.

When I took on this client, I had a feeling our work together would go this way, but my love for the zeros on the proposal nudged me to sign on for a project I wouldn't enjoy and almost dreaded doing. Call it woman's intuition or years of experience, but from our initial meeting, I knew this leader was just blowing smoke and wasn't actually interested in making any changes to his division.

That morning meeting turned out to be a grueling four hours, during which I had to force my face to look like I was paying attention. I faked interest in what they were saying, but I had tuned out, zoned out, and mentally left the conference room. Completely on autopilot, I went through the motions, exactly what I was being paid to do, with no expectation that anything I said or did would make a difference.

Something shifted for me that day. I experienced an epiphany. No longer would I work with clients just for money. Instead, I would have a new level of integrity in my business dealings and align my purpose with profit. I would honor my gifts, and I would fulfill the plan God had for me. It's hard to explain the feeling that came over me, but I knew, at that very moment, my life was shifting into purpose. My life was catapulting to new heights in my business and my personal life. My quest for an authentic business life had officially begun.

This journey of finding myself, finding love, separating from my family, reuniting, growing a purposeful business, nearly losing my marriage, and coming together with my husband again taught me the importance of always dreaming and believing. Throughout this process, I've always felt there was something greater in store for my life.

Even though I lived for years in a toxic relationship and made decisions that ultimately led me to prison, I can look back to find all the positive things in that experience. I can glean wisdom from the bad choices I made. This journey has taught me to trust myself, always know my worth, believe in true love, and know there are good men out there. (Even though society says there are no good Black men, I'm here to tell you there are.)

Many years ago, when my girlfriend experienced a miscarriage, I told her I could never survive that. Lo and behold, I had three (one more recently), and with God's help, I made it through. Through those dark moments I learned you never know what hand life will deal you. All you can do is take it one day at a time.

Prison taught me I'm stronger than I think, and so are we all. Many nights at the camp, I wondered how long my stay was going to last, and I prayed for God to give me an early release. Every time the church doors opened, I was there. Every time there was a revival, I was there. Every time the news reported reduced federal prison sentences, I was watching. However, God didn't deliver me from it. Instead, He gave me the strength to go through it.

When I look back at my life while I was away from my family, it seems like I'm on the outside looking in at someone else's story. Today, I feel so far removed from it, and yet, I'm thankful not to be a statistic. Almost seventy percent of African American children grow up in households run by single parents. Our marriage made it through, and our children have the gift of both parents in their home.

Those experiences helped shape me into the woman, wife, mother, and business owner I am today. They humbled me and exposed me to people from all walks of life. They increased my patience and perseverance and expanded my compassion exponentially. They also taught me that the seeds you sow *will* reap a harvest.

Joyce Meyer said, "You will reap what you sow but not necessarily where you sow." Many of the seeds I sowed in my previous relationship resulted in the harvest I have today in my husband. I poured into a relationship that depleted me and left me with less than I had when I entered it. But from those ashes came the beauty of finding my husband and finding myself. Years spent in an unhealthy relationship positioned me to do what it takes to have the marriage and family I desire. When I lost track of what mattered most, the relationship with God I'd established in my darkest hours allowed me to hear His voice and find my way back again, and the marriage I came so close to losing was saved.

Don't get weary when you're not seeing the harvest where you planted the seeds. Rest assured the harvest will show up in your life, often when you least expect it. It's possible for you to go through hardships of abuse, infidelity, bankruptcy, molestation, divorce, a failed business, abortions, prison, and failures of any kind, and still start anew. I say start anew instead of start over because you've gained wisdom from every situation you've gone through. Therefore, every experience you had is a lesson you can use to start *a new* life today. I pray abundance, peace, and love over your life.

The whole point of being alive is to evolve into the complete person you were intended to be.

_____

OPRAH WINFREY

Chapter 29
Your Personal Evolution

W hile I've left you with my happy ending, it's not the end, and I have not made it yet. I'm continuing to evolve. I'm open to the process and to being honest when I get it wrong. I'm willing to hold a mirror up to my face and study what I see there. I no longer ask for what I think people will give me; I ask for what I want. I'm confident in myself, so I don't have to compete with anyone. Instead, I seek opportunities to collaborate. Rather than judge from a place of insecurity, I support and motivate other women. This is the transparent, unfiltered, makeup-free, not-photo-shoot-ready truth about what it takes to live your life on your own terms while striving to have a successful business, a successful marriage, and a successful family.

Life isn't always going to be neat and easy. Sometimes it's messy, inconvenient, and uncomfortable. Be thankful for where you are because it could always be worse. When I start feeling or acting ungrateful, I think back on my lonely nights, hours spent missing my husband and kids and not being able to do one thing about it. Freedom was so close, yet so far and out of my reach. The bad thing about it was I had neither physical freedom nor mental freedom. I was bound up all the way around and didn't even know it.

Often, your purpose will be birthed out of your pain. It's not unusual to find your calling in the most difficult times in your life. This happened for me. When I was in my darkest valley, I began evolving. What I know for sure is if you have breath in your body, you have all you need to design the life you desire.

Contrary to what much of society tries to tell you, living a happy and abundant life is not just about money. Contentment and wealth are found in a life of peace, loving yourself, and no longer being held hostage by your past. Isn't it time for you to take a step forward to accomplish your dreams? Make a decision today to live free from your past and intentionally design the life you desire.

Decide you're ready to stop talking about what you want in life, and create a plan to go get it. I wholeheartedly believe in creating a safe, trusting, and nonjudgmental space to help women craft a life success plan that propels them into an abundant life.

Let me ask you something.

Are you a high-achieving woman, but there's something missing in your life?

If you're reading this book, your life probably looks great from the outside. But underneath it all, you're ready for your own evolution. You want a life of peace and purpose, but you can't figure out how to make it happen for you.

You wonder *how* you're going to heal from your past.

You worry about *how* you'll grow your business.

You're trying to figure out *how* to improve your marriage.

And all this focus on *how* leaves you feeling completely overwhelmed.

Here's the truth. Before you can figure out how, you need to understand *who* can help you through this process and *why* you must evolve.

If you were drawn to this book, and you identify with my story and feel my energy through these pages, I'm probably your *who*.

There are four phases in the process of evolving: resistance, awareness, reflection, and action. I developed an acronym for EVOLVE to help you understand the process better. Remember this isn't a one-time event it's a lifelong process.

Evaluate areas that need to be healed.

Validate your vision and values.

Open your soul to forgiveness.

Learn how to re-parent yourself.

Value your self-care practice.

Engage in healthy relationships.

Let's start your healing journey together by assessing where you are in your process.

Visit **theceolife.com** to access free resources to discover exactly where you are on your evolving journey and what your next steps can be.

I am here to help you create 360-degree abundance in every area of your life: mind, body, spirit, relationships, finances, and businesses. You don't have to go on this journey alone. The CEO Life motto is "no CEO left behind." Even if you're a professional woman, you're still the CEO of your life. I look forward to helping you evolve from the inside out.

As soon as I became clear that my success as a CEO was directly tied to my success as a wife and mother, abundance followed effortlessly.

T. RENEÉ SMITH

Epilogue
Sending Love and Light

It was a typical afternoon, two years into the pandemic, a time when the world seemed to be headed in the direction of opening back up for good. My younger son and I were talking about his day, and I asked him what book he'd read in school. He looked at me and said, "My mommy is going to have a baby."

"Is that a book you read?" I asked, but he didn't answer. Instead, he walked away and headed upstairs. That was it, nothing more. My son is a little man of few words, so when he says something, I listen.

My husband had commented that I might be pregnant because I'd been so tired over recent weeks, but I hadn't paid much attention. However, after my talk with our son, I went in my bathroom and took an old, expired pregnancy test. I was shocked when I saw two lines that confirmed I was pregnant.

The next morning, I went to the store to get a test that wasn't expired. It came back positive. I took one a few days later, and it came back positive too.

I had stopped birth control years earlier and hadn't gotten pregnant, so I wasn't sure I could still conceive. It took me a few days to just take everything in. Finally, I called the doctor and scheduled my first prenatal appointment. I started taking my prenatal vitamins and took naps when I was tired, but about a week and a half from the day of that first test, I woke up and discovered I was bleeding.

At first, it was a little spotting, so I thought it was implementation bleeding. However, as the day progressed, the bleeding grew heavier. To my surprise, I didn't feel nervous or concerned. I was calm and hopeful. The bleeding continued for a few days, so I called my doctor's office. Since I was so early in the pregnancy, the nurse explained, it would be hard to detect anything right now, and I should keep my scheduled appointment three days later.

His suspicions aroused, my husband asked me if I was pregnant, and I told him I was, but I was bleeding. Anthony was supportive and reassuring, but I wanted to process whatever the doctor said on my own, so I didn't ask my husband to come with me to my appointment.

At the doctor's office, the nurse was friendly and comforting. When the doctor came in and reviewed my results, she told me my urine sample only showed a small amount of the pregnancy hormone HCG. She checked my uterus, and it was open, indicating a likely miscarriage. I completed blood work to confirm the pregnancy loss and left.

I immediately called my husband, and he continued to offer his love and support. Our oldest son was celebrating his birthday that weekend with a sleepover and a fun-filled day at the trampoline park, and Anthony asked if I wanted to re-schedule. Even though there was a lot going on, I chose not to move the party date. Just the day before, we'd celebrated our fifteenth wedding anniversary at Chef G. Garvin's LowCountry Steakhouse, and a mere twenty-four hours later, my dreams of welcoming my little angel into the world had vanished.

Over the weekend, I enjoyed my son's friends, laughed with my husband, and continued to process how I was feeling. I took a healing bath with Epsom salts and essential oils and played healing music, and I felt calm and relaxed. A sense of peace filled the space where I might have expected to feel sadness and loss.

I didn't know if this was a delay or a denial from God, but as I processed everything, I chose to surrender it all to Him. I chose not to ask why this happened to me and not to be angry. I chose instead to ask what lesson I was supposed to learn.

As I saw pregnant women everywhere I turned, whether in the grocery store, on the street, or online (I swear every other picture in my Instagram feed was of an adorable baby girl), I chose to say a prayer for the mothers and their unborn children. I blessed them and sent love and light. I chose to be thankful that, in my mid-forties, I was able to get pregnant naturally. Rather than go into a state of despair, I stayed in a space of gratitude and acceptance of God's will.

This didn't just happen. I was intentional about meditat-ing, praying, and worshipping. I focused on staying in a place of faith rather than giving myself a big pity party and inviting all my friends. I made a conscious decision not to tell anybody about the miscarriage except my husband, my best girlfriend, and my therapist, who helped me process everything. I didn't want other people projecting their opinions and feelings on me.

I listened to many sermons from T. D. Jakes and other pastors about faith, surrendering, being in the wilderness, and trusting God. My girlfriend reminded me that if you don't have tests, then you'll never know how much you've grown. I was able to see my growth during this process as I continued to evolve into a woman of resilience, faith, and compassion.

Sending love and light to my dearest little daughter angel. I hope to meet you soon. If not, your spirit is forever with me. Mommy loves you.

About T. Reneé Smith

Business and Life Strategist T. Reneé Smith started her first business at age nineteen—on credit, with no business experience and no plan. She built a successful enterprise, but later was forced to file bankruptcy and build her new business from the ground up.

Now a reformed people pleaser, ex-perfectionist, and recovered workaholic, T. Reneé uses the lessons she has learned from her more than twenty-eight years in business and more than fifteen years as a wife and mother to empower women to create harmony in their marriage, family, and business. Her life philosophy is simple: Live life on your own terms. Design a life that you love, full of peace, purpose, and prosperity,

LET'S STAY CONNECTED!

T. Reneé Smith

Join **The Evolving Woman**
private Facebook group at:
facebook.com/groups/evolvewithtrenee

Receive your complimentary training resources
and assessments by visiting:
treneesmith.com

Connect with me on social media:
@coachtrenee
@ceolifenation

Follow the hashtag:
#CoachTRenee
#Evolving
#HealTheInnerCEO
#TheCEOLife

If you benefited from this book, please leave a review on **Amazon.com**!

Remember success is your birthright. It's time for you to evolve so you can experience 360-degree abundance in every area of your life.

Made in the USA
Columbia, SC
04 July 2024

38097401R00143